CRASH COURSE

Crash Course

BERNIE BULKIN

**One year to become a great
leader of a great company**

First published in Great Britain in 2015 by
whitefox publishing ltd.
www.wearewhitefox.com

1 3 5 7 9 8 6 4 2

ISBN (TPB): 978-0-9930910-5-6
ISBN (e-book): 978-0-9930910-4-9

Typeset in Sabon and Trade Gothic by Birdy Book Design

Printed in Great Britain by Clays Ltd., St Ives plc

For Jacob, Samantha, Benjamin and Nathaniel
who will lead in the second half of this century

Wake, butterfly –
it is late, we have miles
to go together
BASHO

Table of Contents

WINTER   5

'Twice a week the winter thorough, here stood I to keep the goal'
HOUSMAN

SPRING 67

'Blossom by blossom the spring begins'
SWINBURNE

SUMMER 143

'Summer has set in with its usual severity'
COLERIDGE

AUTUMN   215

'O wild west wind, thou breath of autumn's being'
SHELLEY

Thematic Table of Contents

Foreword

Throughout my career, I have always found it difficult to discuss leadership in abstract terms. It is not something which leaders typically try to rationalise in the course of daily business, and it cannot be distilled into a set of rules to be followed. So much depends on the individual in question and on the context in which they are operating. As Bernie admits, accounts of leadership are necessarily biased by the subject's own experiences. I make no apology for my own bias in what follows.

In my experience, when it comes to leadership, there are just two things which set the best leaders apart from the rest of the pack. The first is the ability to assemble great teams and to provide them with an inclusive working environment. It is the responsibility of a leader to put the right people, with the right skills, in the right place, each with an equal voice. If any one link in that chain breaks down, then so too will a company's ability to execute its leader's strategy. Every CEO says that their people are their most important asset, but very few spend their most important time on managing those people.

The greatest leaders are also ably to defy the German philosopher Hegel, who wrote that 'what history teaches us is that people . . . have never learned anything from history.' In my experience, the only way to learn from the past is continually to tell stories, in particular stories of failure. A willingness to embrace failure demonstrates clear-eyed realism about the challenges an organisation faces, and will instantly build a leader's credibility. Stories of success inspire people, but stories of failure are the most effective mechanism for learning, and they need not be confined to the professional sphere. If told again and again, stories become part of an organisation's history. They add an emotional element to the rationality of business, and generate role models which provide an example for others to follow or to avoid. Leaders are the curators of these stories, and it is their responsibility to share them and to pass them on.

In *Crash Course*, Bernie has done just that. This collection of stories should serve not as a prescription for others to copy or to follow, but as inspiration which leaders can apply to their own circumstances. The more I think about leadership, the more I think about the ways in which personal success and failure impact on the psychology of a leader. In my experience, it is unsustainable for a leader permanently to separate their personal and professional lives, so Bernie has wisely embraced both halves of his life in this book. *Crash Course* demonstrates that there really is no such thing as a book on leadership; there are only stories. It is an outstanding contribution to the study of leadership, from an outstanding scientist, author and leader.

Lord Browne of Madingley

Preface – the idea of this book

Many of us aspire to leadership roles, but when we get them we have no time to learn how to do the job. Trained as scientists and engineers, finance guys, inventors or lawyers, we pick up things by watching others, sometimes good techniques, sometimes terrible, or we learn by trial and catastrophic error. In a big company, you might have had the chance to go on one or two courses, forgetting most of the content before you ever got back to the office. Even so, most of those courses focus on personal development, and don't seem to mention how to make a company more effective, more distinctive, and more powerful in its industry.

We all need a crash course in how to be effective leaders. This book gives you that in two ways. There are 52 short essays, one a week, 13 for each season. Read one on Monday morning, start to practise it that day, and continue to refine and hone your internal dos and don'ts. At the end of the year you will be more assured, *and* your organisation will perform at a higher level. The essays cover skills (sure, these seem basic, but it is amazing how many times, if you are observant, poor performance on these fundamentals is evident in the leaders you see), careers, teams and people, business process, and strategy. You need to be pulling yourself up on all these fronts at once, so in every season there is a selection from each category.

And then we can learn from all of our life experiences to make ourselves better leaders. No, not the daily routine, but the extraordinary things that we are all given a chance to do from time to time. Jury service; travelling to India, Russia, Uzbekistan; buying and selling houses; learning a new physical skill like archery or horseback riding. This starts when we are children, because great schools (tough schools even) produce great leaders, leaders who are determined risk takers. Through our experiences, if we use them properly to learn lessons, we get better and better.

So while every Monday there is a new competency or skill to add to the leadership repertoire, from time to time at the weekend read about some of my life experiences, what I have taken from them, and then reflect on your own experiences.

What does it take to lead in the modern firm? Strategic thinking, of course. But that is far from enough. Just as important is an ability to execute that strategy. So leadership requires competency to make the firm work to deliver tough targets. It is about ensuring alignment at all levels. That takes an understanding of people, a talent to build the best teams, and it takes a high level of personal performance across a range of competencies. Leadership is about sensitivity to the environment (broadly defined), and the sorts of relationships that a firm needs to develop if it is to succeed. Ultimately, leadership is also about understanding how to make you and your company distinctive, separate from the pack fighting for the attention of investors, customers, and the best new employees.

These essays are about many aspects of the leader in the modern firm. They have their foundation in my experiences close to the heart of a large corporation, BP, as it went through a remarkable series of transformations. Indeed, BP went from being played by the markets and its competitors, to being the company that had a big say in determining what the game was. This book aims to give you the insights I derived from my experiences and observations so that you can effect this sort of change in positioning with your company.

The transformation of BP was driven by three successive CEOs. First, the late Bob Horton, who, fresh from a few years in the US, instituted a radical cultural change called Project 1990. He saw the problem, the need to sweep away a lot of old ways of working, but soon found himself enmeshed in a number of crises of his own making. I was among those looking on and wondering, 'Did he really just do that?' In 1992 David Simon became CEO, and began rebuilding the firm's financial and strategic base. He found simple ways of stating performance goals, motivating employees and reassuring investors. Finally, in the second half of the decade and into the new millennium, John Browne built upon the recovery, and transformed BP from a solid middleweight to a heavyweight, leading not just BP but a reconfiguration of the oil industry. Following mergers, acquisitions, and divestments that included Amoco, Arco, Mobil Europe, Castrol, part of Solvay, Veba, and others, the company at the end of his tenure was unrecognisable from the one at the beginning.

And yet throughout there was a thread, a logic – a logic of building on what had gone before, constant strategic positioning, making mistakes and learning from them – until eventually strategy and organisational design were dynamic processes deeply embedded in the leadership. Change happened frequently; yes, it was frightening to some and disruptive to many, but it meant that this was a company which did not stand still; it was relentless in trying to find a better way to do the job.

During the evolution of the company, I saw a transformation in how it developed and treated people. BP in the 1990s became what it had not been before: a rigorous meritocracy, a place where people of high calibre were sought, tested, and rewarded. The importance of the leadership of the company became very clear – not just the top five or six, but the top 40–50, and the senior 300 as well. By investing time in the alignment of the senior leadership it was possible to achieve alignment across the corporation. And by investing in the processes to select the leadership, the aspiration of the best people to be part of that team was reinforced.

Of course, no company is perfect. Sometimes it stumbles, and if it is a big company it has the possibility of making some big mistakes. BP developed tremendous confidence, and there came a point in 2004–06 where that confidence seemed to me to become less a sound foundation and more a danger of weakening what underpinned the company. Some big problems occurred, and the leadership had to move aggressively to deal with them. It did not always do this in a sure-footed way.

The essays in this book are my attempt to capture some of the lessons, the approaches, the skills, the competencies, the dangers, the mistakes that I saw on the way, and to do so in a simple, easy to read, uncomplicated way. The book is biased. It is about what I learned as a dedicated observer and participant in one company, which was a tough school. And it is biased as well by my experiences of being a juror on a gang murder trial, of growing up on the streets in the East New York neighbourhood of Brooklyn, of buying my first house, of seeing how any system can be undermined by its employees, be they in the Soviet Union or British Telecom.

Since I left BP, I have reflected on what I learned, and have tried to capture some of the lessons in this book. But I continue to work. I have been a director of many companies, large and small, and Chairman of three of them. And in this work I am still learning, and gathering material for the essays that will be the second year of the CRASH COURSE.

About the Author, Age 62

Sometime in 2002 I decided that I needed to leave BP. I had a great job, as Chief Scientist, indeed a great job with a great title to go with it (and titles are important to people). My job had two parts, first, to lead the science and technology input to BP's strategy, which I did jointly – sometimes agreeing, sometimes not, with the Chief Economist, Peter Davies. This took a small amount of my time but turned out to be very important, for my future as well as for the company, because I really immersed myself in energy issues again; second, to figure out what was going on in the world of science that could affect BP on any time scale (now, in the next few years, 15 years on) and in any geography (from Cambridge UK to Cambridge USA, to Moscow to Beijing) figure out what we should do about it, and then do it. I had the freedom and the influence to think about how biology could impact our company, recognizing that we did not have any biologists on the staff, then to go to

MIT and Cambridge and Cal Tech and talk to faculty about whether there was a way we could work on this together, only to find that the thought leaders were completely uninterested in oil companies, thinking that the future for industrial collaboration was only in pharmaceuticals (that would change, very dramatically and very quickly). Having discovered that, I was searching for the possibility of an industrial collaboration when Tom Connolly of DuPont contacted me for a chat, following which I was able to bring together many of the BP research and business leadership, while he brought their counterparts from DuPont, and we met for days in New York to hammer out a collaboration which still continues as a business joint venture today. This is just one of many examples of interesting and high impact activities I did as Chief Scientist.

Why leave then, when I still had plenty to do and plenty of energy to do it? When, in fact, the company is structured so that it is much more financially advantageous to be made redundant than to resign or retire (a very stupid structure, by the way). As I thought and thought about this, there were several good reasons to leave. Besides the great parts of my job, I had to go to lots of meetings, all over the world, often with the technology leadership of the company, or its advisors, and I found that many of these meetings were becoming boring. I was spending days on airplanes and sitting in hotel meeting rooms in Houston or Chicago, participating, but wanting to be someplace else. When I get bored I don't go to sleep, I become destructive, cynical (do you recognise this behaviour?). Second, something in my mind said that it is best not to overstay your welcome. I had had a great career, I felt liked and respected in the company after a rough period some years before, so why not leave rather than wait until someone felt the need to push me out? Third, although I had no idea what I would do next, I knew that within BP there was no real possibility of doing something different to what I was doing. The company had found a slot where I was comfortable and it was comfortable with me. I would not get another challenging assignment. I wanted a chance to test myself in different ways, and BP would not give me that chance. And then I had an urge to write down some of the things I had learned from watching great leaders, and some not so great leaders.

Still, it is so comfortable once you have earned a respected position inside a big company. I knew everyone; I knew how to make things happen. And my basic needs were well taken care of. If I had to travel to Moscow for three days, Sandra prepared an itinerary that anticipated what would happen hour by hour – who would take me to the airport, who would meet me at the other end, the hotel, the local drivers, all the way until I was back safe in my own little bed in London. And if a driver didn't turn up on time, I had a phone numbers to find him or her. Of course she made a second copy for my wife as well.

One day not long before I left BP I came down from my office to go to a lunch, and as I was leaving the building I realised that it had started to rain, and I hadn't brought my umbrella. I turned to go back, and the doorman at 1 St James' Square handed me an umbrella. 'There you are, sir,' he said. As I strolled down to Pall Mall I thought, 'My

God, I don't even have to remember my umbrella. How will I manage?'

WINTER

'Twice a week the winter thorough,
here stood I to keep the goal'

HOUSMAN

WEEK 1

The Abuse of PowerPoint

In some ways, the invention of PowerPoint, and of projectors to show computer generated slides, was a great thing. In my professional lifetime I have moved from presentations using glass lantern slides, with all the lettering drawn by hand using special ink and lettering devices, to 35mm slides prepared a week or two in advance of a presentation, to overhead transparencies that could be made more or less up to the last minute (but where the quality of anything but typed material was pretty marginal), to the computer generated slide.

Now we can show charts and graphs, photographs, interactive spreadsheets, animation – in short we can take a presentation relying on words and bring it to life. Great. So how do most presenters use this new facility? By making slide after slide of words, bulleted lists – the most boring slides imaginable.

Why do we do this? To some extent, slides have always

been a crutch for the weak communicator ('even if they can't hear or understand me, they can at least read the message') – as if people would like to assemble somewhere to read as a group – and for the speaker who does not really know his subject well enough to talk it through convincingly. PowerPoint seems to have added to these two weak justifications for slides the ability to prepare a talk at the last minute. Which, believe it or not, always comes out sounding like a talk prepared at the last minute.

Academics love to use slides, and their professional life is recorded on their slide collections. Somehow this tendency has pervaded industry. When I first came from a university post to work at Standard Oil of Ohio, I was asked to speak as part of a presentation to senior management of the company about the impact that emerging computer technology would have on the business. I duly prepared 45 (really, 45!) slides to show, and thought they made a nice logical flow. Ten minutes after completing a rehearsal in front of our vice president, he appeared in my office and said, 'That was so bad I didn't know where to start', and as we spoke he showed me how I could do a more powerful presentation with three slides. I never looked back.

There is an exception to this approach, and that is when many in the audience are non-native speakers of the language of the presentation. So if I am speaking in English in China, or Russia, or Argentina, I always want a full slide pack with words making the major points, because non-native speakers will have the reinforcement of reading with listening, and will not fall behind through trying to understand what point I was trying to make.

If you have any doubts about the potential for freeing yourself from PowerPoint, I have two suggestions. First, try to do a slideless presentation. Think about the four points you are going to make in a talk and how you are going to make them powerfully without slides. Then think about where you need to show something increasing or decreasing, and how that requires a graph. Think about shares that might require a pie chart. Or about how a photograph will convey beauty, ugliness, or scale. Second, read the little pamphlet by Edward Tufte called 'The Cognitive Style of PowerPoint' (available from www.edwardtufte.com), which also addresses some of the bad graphical approaches available in PowerPoint.

When you have thought about it in this way, I suggest you start your preparation for a presentation, especially to a senior group with: No slides, just talk. Then add back any slides with visual information that you are struggling to convey with words. If you do this, you will often find yourself giving talks with no slides; many times, if there are several presentations being made in the meeting, you will be the exception, which is even better. Imagine the relief of, and the impact on, a senior executive group that has sat through several batteries of slides, when you come in, sit down, and just talk to them directly.

WEEK 2

Let Me Read You a Speech

'But in a larger sense, we cannot dedicate, we cannot consecrate, we cannot hallow this ground.'

'That government of the people, by the people, for the people shall not perish from the earth.'

Lincoln's Gettysburg Address

It might appear that nothing is easier than having a speech all typed out in front of you (or in Lincoln's case written out by his own hand), and getting up to read it. In fact, it is probably the most difficult way to give an effective speech.

The written word and the spoken word are very different. Just try listening to a talking book, especially a non-fiction work, and think about how you concentrate on that compared to listening to a really good speaker. The difference is clear. When we are giving a good speech, we use rhetoric. Churchill and Lincoln were great practitioners of this. Listen to some of their speeches and you will see how effectively they hook you in. But if you read this stuff in a book you would think it phony and over-inflated. By contrast, there are people who write speeches as if they were student essays, with complex sentences that could be followed if you were reading them but are incomprehensible to you as a listener.

When you sit down to write a speech, you have to be writing for speaking, not writing for reading. You have to hear it in your own voice. We are each of us different in how we speak, how loud or how soft, how comfortable we are with flourishes and alliteration, what words or phrases we like, what makes us cringe. And this needs to be at very front of mind when writing a speech.

Now we come to a little problem. Executives often don't write their own speeches. In many companies there are individuals whose job it is to at least get the first draft, or even the final version of a speech ready. So how can you get the voice right in that situation?

Well, it is easy to spot when it goes wrong. I often see this with speeches given by Ministers in the UK Government. Ministers give a lot of speeches, and accept a lot of speaking engagements, especially in London. I have heard many speeches which have all the right points and sentiments in them, but they were written for the minister by a civil servant, and because of the press of time only looked at in the car going over from the office to the speaking location. The result: A flat delivery, sounding every bit like what it is, someone else's words being read out with insufficient preparation.

This approach can never be made to work; I don't care how talented you are. Here is what does work for a speech written by someone else: First, sit down with the speech-writer a couple of weeks in advance. Talk through the points together, so that she can hear them from you in your own words. If the writer is any good, they will come prepared with ideas for talking points, and the discussion of those will sharpen what is going to be said.

Step two is to read through a draft, say a week in advance, and as you read it make changes to put in or eliminate phrases. As you are doing this, think about saying the words yourself, just as I have discussed in Week 11. This Speech is on These Note Cards. Then move to a final draft.

And finally you need to make time to read through the whole thing before giving the speech, again making changes in the final draft. The whole process is one of getting it more and more into your own voice. I keep making changes to speeches I have written myself right up until the last few minutes before I have to go up to the podium. Indeed, I am often surprised about how frequently awkward wording creeps into the written speech. While I am reading through, my pen is putting in prominent commas and other punctuation to help me with my phrasing, timing and breathing.

Now for the delivery. A good speech needs to be delivered with emotion, with passion, like you actually believe what you are talking about. And I hope that you do! Otherwise it is junk, it will sound like junk, and the audience will put it in that place in their brain where they store other junk.

WEEK 3

Building Best Teams – Part 1

In the very centre of BP's chart of competencies (Week 41. Competencies and Skills) for the leadership of the corporation is 'Builds Best Teams'. I suppose we would all salute that one, yes, sure, best teams; of course you have to be able to do that. But what does it mean? And how do you go about it?

I started to think about this before the BP competency framework ever saw light of day; I suspect that most people who aspire to leadership think a lot about how to build a 'best team' in whatever management role they have. When I first thought about this I was leading something called the Oil Division at the BP Research Centre. We had about 15 research teams, and the leaders of these teams, plus a few other key individuals in staff roles, more or less constituted my leadership team to accomplish something of value for the corporation.

When I talked with the Team Leaders, and also with my

insightful HR director for the Division, it was clear that although we used the word 'team' a lot, we had not given any thought to what it meant, or whether we were a leadership team, a collection of research teams, or perhaps we were just a few hundred people, with specific projects and skills, coming in to work to do our jobs every day – something very different.

So I had an idea. Why not get someone really successful from one of the major football (soccer) clubs here in the UK to come and talk to my leadership 'team' about how to achieve really high performance. At that time, George Graham was the leader of Arsenal Football Club, and was among the most successful managers in the league. I wanted to know, what does he do to achieve this sort of success? Is it in getting the best players and just letting them do their thing? Or was it inspirational speeches? Or was it something else altogether? What I knew from my much longer history with baseball and football in the US is that there were individuals (such as the late Billy Martin) who moved from one team to another and achieved excellent results pretty much wherever they went. I wanted to learn their secrets.

But before I could put this cunning plan into action, I had a call from someone in 'Group Learning' who had heard of my interest. 'Great,' I said, 'how do I get George Graham over here?' 'Well, interesting idea,' he responded, 'but perhaps I can suggest a better idea. We recently met some sports psychologists named John Syer and Christopher Connolly, and they have been working with athletes at successful football teams, and also with business. Why don't you give them a try, because we think they actually understand this business of team building better than most people?'

So here is a first lesson on how to build best teams: get some professional help. Yes, you can have good instincts about what to do, and using these instincts you can have some success. But pros like John and Christopher have a lot of techniques they can use to help you be much more successful.

I took a chunk of money from a tight budget and allocated it to team workshops with these professionals. We started with an afternoon with my leadership team, a taster session. When that ended, I am sure that some of the crusty team leaders thought their boss was a madman, but two came up to me and said, 'I want my team to have the first workshop with these guys.'

If I step back from the various exercises we did that afternoon and in many subsequent two-day workshops, and ask what John and Christopher seemed to be trying to accomplish, I think it is this: first, the team members need to get to know each other better. It may not be a characteristic of teams everywhere, but it certainly was the case for us that people could work together every day for years and not know very much about one another. This slight deepening of knowledge is the beginning of finding new ways to motivate 'stretch performance', performance by the team beyond what any of the individuals believe is possible.

Second, we needed new ways of talking to one another. They recognized that all of us slip into ways of speaking that are vague, evasive, and indirect. But more important, better ways of one-to-one communication can be learned, and that that learning, if practised, can be quite enduring.

Third, in every existing team there are problems, between individuals, between the leader and some or all of the team members, and between the team and the organisation in which it sits. With professional help, these problems can be surfaced in a controlled way, explored, sometimes dealt with or even resolved. But even when there is no resolution, a professional guided exploration of the problem is helpful.

I was very struck by this last point and its effectiveness, and remain convinced that, if you can afford it, the team building workshop using professionals is one of the best investments you can make. By contrast, if you feel that team building is necessary and can't afford the investment to do it right, you need to be very careful about what is done. In particular, surfacing problems with only amateur help can make things a lot worse than they were when the problems were buried.

There are still exercises that you can learn, and do, that will help the team to forge stronger links and strive for higher performance. Insist that your HR manager offers you such exercises, trains you in how to use them and gives you feedback. Achieving team performance beyond what you and your team members thought possible is so important and so rewarding that it must demand your attention.

WEEK 4

Having Fun Yet?

Gary Grieve, who was my predecessor in my job as Director of Manufacturing and Supply, and who had many different managerial roles in the company, had a slide that he showed to a new group he was leading. It looked something like this:

Objectives for 2010
1. Make money
2. Have fun (optional)

What is the place of fun in the leadership of a corporation? Is it fun when the one-third of participants in a company conference who are dedicated golfers go off to play, leaving the rest of us to lounge around the hotel? Is a night at the pub putting away several pints of beer fun? Is fun actually optional, and if so for whom?

I have been to some 'fun' events at corporate meetings

that were definitely not fun. A carefully planned karaoke evening that was positively painful, for example. Or some boat trips that seemed to go on forever with very little purpose or fun.

Still, it is possible to mix fun with business. Not long ago, I was with a company board in Shanghai, when, following a long day of meetings, intense discussions and a dinner with staff, someone suggested the entire board go for foot massages at 1 am, and we all just loved it.

Fun can be planned, but it really works when the team feels like doing it. I was once with a group of executives in a hotel somewhere in Penang for a couple of days, just on the edge of a lake, and finally someone said, 'This windowless room and this air conditioning is getting to me, let's take a little time off and get out in the fresh air.' So a boat was arranged to cruise around the lake, and we worked, ate, drank, swam, worked some more – we had all our meetings for a day on the boat. And the meeting became a memorable one both because of what we accomplished and how we accomplished it.

The role of fun is, at any time, a test of the sensitivity of the leader and of the team members as to what is appropriate, and what will lift spirits. It can be a day at the races, or some outdoor games (I have good memories of such things as blindfold Land Rover driving or human sheep dog trials). But I have those good memories, in contrast to my bad ones of the karaoke evening, because someone read the state of the team just right on those days.

And one other point. There is a time to cancel fun activities. We were holding a meeting when word came of an accident involving a company ship on which there were fatalities. That was not a night to take the whole team out on the town, as was planned. Better a quiet dinner, a nightcap, and to bed.

WEEK 5

Decommoditising Your Business

Do you think it would be great if you could wake up each morning, pick up the daily newspaper off your doorstep, turn to the financial pages, and check a table to see how much money your company made yesterday? If you do, then you are probably thinking about your company's product as a tradable commodity, with little in your business to differentiate yourself from others selling that commodity. If that is your business model, you are probably set for returns that range from average to poor. Such is the nature of commodity businesses.

So if you are in a business, whose major product is a commodity, you need a strategy for decommoditising. One of the most original thinkers on this subject is Henry Weil of MIT. He put forward several possible strategies, including:

- Reduce the amount of capital you have employed in the business – this gives you more flexibility to respond to changes in markets;

- Have dramatically lower costs than your competitors – opening up possibilities for adding back costs that allow differentiation;

- Bundle services with the commodity product – which means understanding who your customers are and what they need; even saying the word 'customer' is a triumph for many in commodity businesses;

- Take the moral high ground on key issues – make people want to be your customers because of what you stand for.

BP has used all of these strategies, and you can find ways of using them in your own company. Indeed, you must find ways of doing that if you are going to be successful. BP started by looking at its products – crude oil, refined products, retailing of gasoline, and petrochemicals – and realising that all of these were thought of as commodity businesses. If you find this in your own company, you must make a transition to the idea that your goal as a business, any part of the business, is to figure out how to be *distinctive* in your sector. Example: We explore for oil, others explore for oil. There was a time when BP was producing oil from some large fields in the North Sea and Alaska, and small fields in any number of countries around the world. In this its profile was similar to Shell, Exxon, Mobil and others. Certainly it was not distinctive. The leadership asked how to make oil production distinctive, and settled on a strategy of exploring and investing in production only in places where large fields were possible – a strategy of finding elephants. Is there not a similar strategy needed for sellers of paracetamol, granola, or solar panels?

But the crude oil produced is still a commodity, you say. It still goes into the market where you can see its price on the front page of the paper every day. OK, but the crudes being produced get different values compared to benchmark crude oils, the well-known Brent and West Texas Intermediate, for example. So the group in the company that is responsible for bringing the crude oil to market needs what? A marketing team, of course. A team that establishes the quality of a new crude oil, why it should command a superior price vis à vis the benchmark, that convinces refineries of other companies that this is crude oil they want to get. In other words, a distinctive process that decommoditises the product as far as the customers are concerned.

If you can exercise control over an asset without owning 100% of it, or if you can use other people's money, giving them a fair return, if you can find ways of maintaining control over your free cash flow, if you can acquire assets so that they come onto the books with low capital employed, then you have flexibility. BP found ways of doing this with refineries, and a lot of opportunistic independent refiners found ways of acquiring assets from major oil companies like BP for little more than the working capital, thus gaining an advantaged position in a commodity business – as long as the market measure of success was return on capital employed.

One defining leadership technique is to be relentless about cost reduction (see Week 38. Cost Cutting as a Never Ending Process). Anything is a good excuse for cutting costs. Low oil prices, let's cut costs. High oil prices, let's be clear that we are not using this as an excuse to let costs run wild. Merger? We have to take out costs in all overlap areas to make it successful, but let's use this time to re-examine costs in other areas as well. Exxon does this really well.

Bundling services doesn't always work, but when it does, it really does. Air BP is a great example of this. Their product is Jet Fuel, and this is almost the ultimate commodity, traded in liquid markets, and so tightly specified that there is no opportunity for product differentiation. So what does Air BP do? First it recognises that how it participates in logistics at the airport is a differentiator. It asks how we can train our customers in safety or checking the fuel quality. This is a service the company can sell with the fuel. Second, it realises that the business is not about the fuel, but about credit terms for buying the fuel – that different airlines have different credit worthiness, leading to different terms, but if you are a big global player you are internally hedging some of that credit risk, in a way that many of your smaller competitors could not.

Finally, taking the moral high ground. Again, it doesn't always work, but when it does, oh boy! BP did this on climate change, on cleaner fuels, on political donations. You almost always have to do it first to get the full impact, but it does allow you to step away from the pack in a commodity business, especially with the retail customer. But a warning, this has to be about substance, not about an advertising campaign. Indeed, advertising is not a strategy for decommoditising, is it?

WEEK 6

False Economy

Cutting costs is for all seasons, but there is a great temptation for overzealous leaders to make decisions which look good but are counterproductive. There are a few ways this can happen. Decisions get made at a high level which should be made lower down, or not at all. Or a senior executive responds to a good sales approach from an alternative supplier, without having a real understanding of what the essential and desirable features of the product or service he is buying, or replacing, really are.

Two examples: Number one, probably once every year or two I heard someone propose that when employees fly on company business, their frequent flyer miles should belong to the company, not to them. Sounds reasonable? After all, the company bought the air ticket. But the insightful executive will know something about how his employees travel. I know that when I was responsible for all the people supporting BP's refineries, my engineers would fly out to

Germany on an early flight, work all day at the refinery, and try to catch the last flight back, sometimes getting back to their homes at 10 or 11 that night. Then they could be at work by 8 am the next morning. Likewise, finishing up a meeting in New York at 6 pm, they would head out to the airport to get the overnight flight back to London, arrive at 6 am, shower at the airport and come into work.

But decide to take away frequent flyer miles, a tiny perk for the weary traveller to use later with her family vacation, and we would encourage a completely different set of behaviours. At the end of a long day, why not check into a local hotel, have dinner, and take a flight the next morning instead?

Number two, the corporation has a contract with a tax firm to assist expatriates and the company with settling US and foreign tax. The contract has run for years, and perhaps it is a little too comfortable. So an executive takes this in hand, lets others compete, and awards the contract to a rival firm with a significantly lower bid. But did he ever think to talk with a selection of expatriates about what they liked or did not like about the existing contract? What aspect of service was most important to the employees, what was of little importance? Suddenly a small aspect of the company's operations goes from ticking quietly along to generating a storm of complaint letters. Instead of getting kudos for saving costs, the executive is in trouble for upsetting key employees trying to do a job in a foreign country, with families who have difficulty adjusting.

So, yes there are savings everywhere. Yes, we have to keep searching out these savings and reviewing all our costs. Yes, we have to challenge our suppliers, including those who have been long-term contractors. But think. Be sensible. Talk to the people affected. You are an executive because you have a brain.

WEEK 7

Flatten, Flatten, Flatten

I know that Tom Peters and others have played this particular song before, but the removal of layers in a corporation must be a never ending theme. There is something about companies that provides a fertile soil for the growing of layers – maybe it is the human instinct to reward those working for us by putting them in charge of someone else.

But it does not do anything for productivity, morale, or making money for there to be people with no other function than to manage other people, who are in turn managing other people . . . As I think Tom Peters once said, just look at a company with a 100 storey headquarters building and you will see a metaphor for the whole corporation – 100 layers of bureaucracy stacked one on top of the other.

Great leaders can deal with having a lot of people reporting to them. It forces them to know a lot about what is actually going on at the front line – what people are working on, what they are succeeding and failing at, what's frustrating them. Insulation may be useful for keeping homes warm and wires shielded, but it has no place in management.

So I believe in stripping out layers. Relentlessly. Find new and productive things for the middle managers to do. If they are really still useful, they should be good individual contributors at a senior level. And that is something that *is* needed. People with experience of the business who can see opportunities, advise and consult. But not managing a layer of managers.

In my early management jobs I was hesitant about doing this, but I rapidly lost this hesitation. One of the early re-organisations I did of the 'layer removal' sort was slowed down because the computer program for drawing organisation charts could not do a flat organisation, it only knew about tree structures with four boxes per level.

I think that for some people even fifteen direct reports are quite manageable. A group that size can meet in a room once a week and set directions, tackle key issues together. A good leader can be conversant with the problems – technical, business, people – of fifteen teams. A great leader can move these problems forward, challenge assumptions, guide and shape performance.

Sure, you will spend a fair chunk of your time in a flat organisation meeting with the people who report to you, and talking through their issues. You will, of necessity, be closer to the problems they face with the people who work for them. If you stir yourself and get out of your office regularly, you can be in the workplace of lots of your people by just going down one level. I think one of the most profound managerial challenges I ever heard was 'When did you last see your boss, talking to your staff, in your staff's workplace?' Well, a flat organisation is the way to make that happen, substantively and frequently.

And once a year you will spend a lot of time doing appraisals. Ten or fifteen appraisals, thinking about them, meeting individually, listening as well as talking probably for 45 minutes to an hour, writing something up, reviewing the feedback. All of this takes time. You will also have a lot of staff development issues to consider, depending on the company, as people move on to other jobs, and new people have to be recruited. But aren't all of these things a big part of how a senior leader adds value to the corporation? I think they are, and hence a good use of time.

In a traditional, hierarchical company, the leader who goes for a flat organisation becomes known as something of a radical. I recall putting out a chart for a very flat organisation as part of a big reorganisation the early 1990s, and one of the older divisional managers made a comment in a large meeting about how the new organisation of my Division was very difficult for him to understand! And the Director, to my delight, answered, 'Well, the people inside that Division seem to understand it, so I don't think it matters much whether you do or not.'

WEEK 8

Clutter

In the same way that a clean desk seems to attract clutter, so a corporation can have lots of bits here, there and everywhere that, at best, don't contribute to efficient operation, keeping some people very busy doing things that are harmless but useless; at worst they get in the way of making crisp decisions. The problem is not that this happens; we all know it happens. The problem is figuring out which parts of our processes are essential, and which parts are clutter.

In the early 1990s, when Bob Horton came back to the UK from the US and became Chairman of BP, he immediately eliminated more than 200 corporate committees. Were they all clutter? No, but Bob (living up to his Hatchet Horton nickname) thought this was a good method for figuring out which committees were needed and which were not. Sure enough, within a couple of years about 10 of them had reappeared. Imagine the time saved for productive work by eliminating 190 committees. I recall one of the managing directors saying, before this radical com-mittee elimination process, that before the year started he had meetings booked in already on 125 days. How could he possibly function effectively for the corporation in a situation like that? I would say this is a pretty good test for any Corporate director to take during a Christmas holiday: look over your calendar for the year and ask 'When am I going to get out to see operations?' 'Do I have enough time to work with people individually?' 'At which of these meet-ings am I adding value?' Be rigorous.

But clutter is not just about committees and meet-ings. One of the biggest issues in corporations is internal charging. The R&D department, or IT, or advertising, is required to get business unit support for its projects. In turn the business units start to break down these projects into smaller and smaller units. Management of them is delegated by the business unit leader to lower and lower levels (probably indicating that there are too many levels anyway). Time sheets are used to book time from each indi-vidual to the projects. Sound familiar? Good system?

Up to a point. But when you find – and you will find this – that someplace there is a building with hundreds of people just running the internal company charging sys-tem, taking a charge for three telephone calls and moving it from internal account A to internal account B, you might ask yourself, 'Isn't there a better way?'

The leader's job is not to challenge every process, rather, it is to be sure that the culture in the company is one of everyone in management challenging processes to be sure they are efficient. With internal charge out systems, someone has to be stepping back and asking 'What are we trying to accomplish here?' and then, 'How can we accomplish this most efficiently?'

Clutter is thus another word for excessive corporate overhead. Clutter is demoralising to everyone, or it should be. Unless the leadership of the company is ruthless in rooting it out, clutter is inevitable and will become a drag on competitiveness.

FOR THE WEEKEND:

Unimpressive Leaders

My friend and colleague Nadia Pallatt was once talking to me about some of those leading our business, and she recommended the last film that Peter Sellers made, *Being There*, about a somewhat mentally challenged gardener who is taken for a wise man as a result of cryptic comments he makes on life. She felt that some of the leaders we were being asked to follow were pretty much in this mould: they knew a few key phrases and when to utter them, but otherwise were fairly ignorant of everything that was going on around them. I had to agree.

Over time, if you hold various senior positions in university or business life, as I have, you meet a large number of chief executives. I don't just mean for a quick handshake, but in a small meeting for, say, half an hour or an hour of discussion. Sometimes it is one on one, sometimes a small group. And after *some* of these meetings I came away with lots to think about, a lot to be impressed with, both on content and process.

But after many other meetings with CEOs it remained a mystery to me about what it could have been that qualified this person for the position they held. I recall many years ago being with Harry Wechsler, a close friend and mentor, who held many senior business positions at Borden and Beatrice Chemical, and we had the opportunity, along with one or two others, to spend an hour with Bill Casey when he was head of the CIA. Casey was a controversial character, lawyer, Republican operative, who had been involved with the OSS, predecessor of the CIA, during World War II. Maybe he was having an off day, maybe he just wasn't interested in talking to us, but the hour was pretty unimpressive as we tried to discuss issues of science, engineering, and world affairs during a turbulent time in world history. When he left, we just looked at each other for a bit, then Harry said, 'Hmm, so that is the Director of the CIA.' That really said it all.

When I was hired by Standard Oil, as a senior recruit, I was scheduled to go and see the Chief Executive, Al Whitehouse. This was interesting in itself, because although I was coming in to a fairly senior position, it was not necessarily close enough to the top that the CEO should see me. I understood afterwards that the reason I got to see him is that he didn't have much else to do, so things like this were arranged to fill his calendar. The business was being run by others. I noticed when I went into his rather grand office that there were no books. On the coffee table around which he and I sat, there was an array of duck hunting magazines.

I think that once Whitehouse established that I had neither experience nor interest in shooting ducks he struggled to find something for us to talk about. Yet this man was the CEO of the 12th biggest company in the US. (Well, not for much longer, as BP showed him the route to the exit the following year.)

This was in great contrast to John Browne, or David Simon, as CEOs of BP. No one ever left a meeting with one of them in any doubt about why they were leading the company. In some cases I saw executives leave doubting their own ability. I once brought the Chief Executive for the UK subsidiary of a major US auto company to see John Browne, as a courtesy really, because we had an alliance with the parent company. Of course I had prepared a briefing note for John about the company this man was leading. Afterwards, John said, 'Thanks for your note. I think I knew more about his business than he did.'

There is something about succession in companies and organisations that can lead to perverse results. Not just the final succession to Chief Executive, but the series of promotions along the way that winnows the field of candidates for the top job, for example selecting them to head a division of the company in a country that is important to the business, like the auto executive. This process should lead to a few excellent candidates, able to run that company or any of a series of other big companies. And that is very often the case. But when the system is broken, when a company doesn't know what competencies it needs at the top, and how to develop these, it winds up with a leader incapable of doing the job. Sometimes it winds up with a leader who is attractive, well dressed, and knows the right phrases to say to the Board or on television, but has not got a clue about how to make a plan, execute a plan, or pick the best people.

Or the Board finds that there is no one in the organisation able to take on the top job. This is a failure, and it is one that must be squarely accepted as a failure by the Board. If they appoint someone unqualified it is because they didn't understand what the company required for the next stage of its life; if they have no suitable candidates, not even one to test against external recruits, then the Board has failed by not paying sufficient attention to succession planning.

In a sense, the single most important lesson of this book is that as you develop your own career in leadership, you should critically observe those you meet in senior executive positions. It is part of your personal job to decide what you admire in them, what puzzles you, and what you find unsatisfactory. Then you must purge yourself of those unsatisfactory behaviours, and build your ability to deliver that which you admire.

WEEK 9

I Do Process, He Does Content

If we look at the jobs of senior management of a corporation, we might ask whether some people are responsible for content, and others process. I had not thought of jobs in this way until someone asked my colleague Tony Meggs, who was Group Vice President for Technology at BP, what he did and what I, as Chief Scientist, did. And he replied, 'Bernie does content, and I do process.'

Hmmm . . . that was interesting. Would anyone really prefer to have their role defined that way, or was he expressing a little jealousy of the fun parts of my job? As it happens, a few years earlier, when I was on the BP Oil Executive Committee, we had a member who often said he was a 'process junkie' and really liked thinking about how we did our business more than about what the business was that we did.

I suppose there is a role for process, and people whose jobs concentrate on it. But I never felt that any job I had was exclusively one or the other, and I don't think that any good leader (and by the way I include Tony in this category) only spends their time on process or only on content.

If you are going to think strategically about the business, you need to do both, and all the time. As I have said in another essay (Week 49.How Jobs Change with Career Progress) as one progresses through a company, one doesn't lose the technical content of one's job, rather one exchanges technical depth for technical breadth. A part of that change is that good leaders must contribute to content as well as process.

Because process is important, great leaders try to innovate on process all the time. Companies that do things a certain way, or are organised a certain way, because that is how they always did it – whether in HR processes, or capital projects, or any of a dozen process areas – are stuck, and in danger of becoming as antiquated in their content as they are in their process. I have seen this happen with a Director of R&D who had been in his position for a decade, who put in place a set of processes when he arrived and didn't change them. The productivity dropped after a few years, but he doggedly kept going.

The great thing about business processes, and for that matter the organisations we put in place to support the processes, are that they are disposable – we try them, we use them, we suck the juice out of them, and then we move on to doing things a new way. Unsettling? Uncomfortable? Of course it is, and all the more reason to try it.

You might argue that certain approaches to business process are very enduring, not disposable at all. For example, each employee needs to have clear objectives, agree these with his or her boss, and be evaluated at least once a year on how he or she has performed against these objectives. The objectives need to be specific, measurable, achievable, and so on. Fine. We can all agree on that.

But what happens next? And what happens also? Are those who did not succeed in meeting their agreed objectives punished, and if so how? Or are they coached, and if so by whom? Is the reward process supportive of the objective setting and appraisal process? How are team objectives set and appraised? Are there letter grades to indicate performance, or do we try to do this with words? There are no correct answers to these questions; there are lots of processes that can be built around even something as fundamental as performance appraisal, reward and grades.

And another example. Most companies have some sort of functional activity outside the business line activity. Who decides on the content of those activities? How is the funding for it accounted for internally? How much is centralised, how much is decentralised to different parts of the business? What is the time horizon of the programme? For all of these things we need process, and it must be process that is clearly understood by both the functional management and the business people. Because if it is not we will not be able to realise the value.

But the processes we have need not be for all times. By changing from a centralised to a decentralised structure we can often strip out programmes that are not of interest to the business. By changing back to a centralised organisation a few years later one can find areas of overlap and duplication, and make better use of skills. Changing processes, viewing existing processes as disposable, is a tool of productivity improvement.

WEEK 10

Four Points

When John Browne starts to speak at a meeting, whether in a speech, or introducing a discussion, or summing up, he often says 'I want to make four points' and all the people who have worked with him for a while will smile, because he almost always has four points. I don't know how he discovered that four was just the right number, but it is one of those simple tricks that can be used extremely effectively.

How many speeches have we all listened to wondering what the point is that the speaker is trying to make? How many times have we seen a chairman unable to draw together the threads of the discussion in a meeting? All too many, I suspect. And many of us have been in this situation ourselves, sometimes giving a speech which seems more like a description of a walk around the garden to see lots of beautiful and interesting flora, than a clear statement of strategy or purpose. (By the way, I have also heard a lot of religious leaders give sermons which suffer from the same deficiency.)

So when I sit down to plan a speech, I simply ask myself 'what are the four points I want to make in this speech?' It doesn't matter if the speech length is 10 minutes or 45 minutes. Four points can be absorbed by the audience, and taken away. They can be stated at the beginning and summarised at the end. The longer speech allows you to elaborate the points, to set out or argue the case, and to illustrate by examples. It is not for adding more and more points.

When you have these four points clear in your own mind, the speech can practically write itself, or if you are using a speech writer, that person can be very clear about how to structure the remarks. And if, as on many occasions, you are speaking from a few notes, being clear about those four points is really all you need.

The same goes for the more dynamic situation that takes place in a meeting. Lots of things are being raised in discussion, but the trick is to tease out the four main points (see also Week 19. Chairing) and summarise these as the meeting is concluding. The value of the meeting, for the executive participants, presenters, and for those recording actions, will be greatly enhanced.

I also use this approach for radio and television interviews. Often there is very little time to prepare, a call comes in, and before long you are in a car on the way to the studio. In the car I take out a pen and a scrap of paper or a business card and think, no matter what questions the interviewer asks, what are the four points I would like to get across in this interview? Somehow it works. Sometimes I only get to two or three of the four, but that is fine.

Of course there are cultural differences. Several years ago, I was on the board of a company doing a lot of business in China, and they asked me to lead a delegation (somehow in China it is always about delegations!) to a meeting with the Chief Technology Officer of Sinopec, a leading Chinese oil and chemicals company. Our guys were trying to get him to sign a licence agreement for our technology. So the day before the meeting, I said to my young Chinese colleagues: 'Think about this, what are the four points you would like me to make in my meeting with Dr Tsao? Write them down, and tell me in the morning.'

The next morning at breakfast they handed me a piece of paper with the four points: 1. Sign the licence agreement. 2. Sign it right now. 3. Pay money up front. 4. A big amount of money.

The four-point method usually works, but not always!

One last caution: do not try this technique in conversation with your spouse.

WEEK 11

This Speech is on These Note Cards

Some people are excellent at speaking from a few notes, or a brief outline. Others find it very difficult. In recent years, people overcome that difficulty by using PowerPoint slides as both their notes and, increasingly, their text. Yet, as I have discussed elsewhere (Week 1. The Abuse of PowerPoint) if you really want to get the attention of your audience you will get rid of your slides, unless they have something to show that is not just words – slides are for graphics, mouths are for words.

The great advantage and disadvantage of speaking from only a few notes are the same: you really have to know what you want to say, and how you are going to say it. And there is nothing as persuasive as a speaker who knows her subject so thoroughly that every bit of it is embedded in her mind.

There are times when speaking from notes, or with neither notes nor slides, is inappropriate. Here are some examples: Doing a briefing for investors, when you want to be sure that you have agreed exactly what you are going to say because the comments can be price sensitive in a public company; speaking to audiences whose native language is different from the language in which you are speaking, and who will be able to digest the subject matter more readily if they can see the words, in which case slides are probably required; formal speeches to large gatherings, or cases where you want to be very smooth in your delivery and not fish for words; talks where you must be very strict on time, and where a text enables you to really time your remarks. (Two extreme examples from my experience: a TV slot we used to do which had to last exactly 55 seconds. Every word had to be carefully chosen, and the pace of speaking those words practised; and the Friday Evening Discourse at the Royal Institution in London, where I was expected to speak for exactly one hour, at which point a bell would sound.)

But notes are a great advantage in many other situations. You convey authority by speaking in a more extemporaneous fashion. You can maintain better contact with your audience than either text or slides allow, because you can be looking around at them all the time, i.e. you can always be 'reading the room'. And you can be flexible enough to respond to things that previous speakers have said, if that is the situation, because you are working from your thoughts rather than from the printed word.

What to do: If I am giving a talk using notes, I start with the same rule I use when writing any speech, namely, 'what are the four points that I am going to make in this talk?' Then I jot down the sub-points I want to be sure to make under each of these. And as I am doing that, I try to be writing very little, but saying aloud or to myself the sentences that I would use to convey the point.

This is very important. If you just have the notes, and have not tried to say it in sentences, both while making the notes and after you have the whole thing down, most people find themselves fumbling for the right word or phrase, and this diminishes the experience that the audience has in listening to you. You are trying to convey the tricky mixture of spontaneity, authority, and audience contact, and to do that you have to be able to concentrate on the audience and their reaction, rather than on finding the right word or phrase.

So talk it through for yourself. And don't try to memorise. That is fatal. It leads to exactly the same sort of problem as not rehearsing at all – you find yourself searching for the way you put it in your memorised text, when several other phrasings will do perfectly well.

Above all, use the speech as an opportunity to understand your subject more deeply. To ask questions, of yourself, of your colleagues and subordinates, to help clarify areas where your depth of understanding is not what it should be. This will also be of enormous help in answering questions.

Here is a last thought that I keep in my mind which applies to speeches generally, however you are giving them. Most of the time, my audience is going to hear presentations from several people, often speaking before me and after me. My personal goal is always for them to leave thinking that mine was the best talk they heard that day. And I want to be self-critical enough to answer myself honestly as to whether I achieved that goal.

WEEK 12

Discrimination

In the modern corporation there is no place for discrimination based on race, gender or sexual orientation. This is an absolute. Any CEO, manager, or team leader who tolerates this abuse, or encourages a culture that fosters it, should be removed. So it is very important for us to understand how it manifests itself, and how deeply this weed sinks its roots once you let it get out of control. But while there is overt discrimination that we would all recognise, there are more subtle forms to which the leader needs to be very alert.

What's so hard about this? I think it is that many of us grew up in a society where policies, practices and attitudes were far from accepting of black people, women, gays, and others, viewing them as less able to assume the same roles as white heterosexual males. When I was growing up in New York City, the high school I attended had many black students, but in the honours classes that I took there were virtually none. Black kids were tough, and, in general, we feared them and stayed out of their neighbourhoods.

My mother, and the mothers of all of my friends, did not work outside the home. A few had been teachers when they were younger, and then stopped working for good when they had children. As we completed high school, the advisers pushed all the boys towards science and engineering, and the girls towards English and the humanities, telling them to make sure they got some sort of school teaching qualification. This pushing was, fortunately, not always very successful, but it was certainly practised.

The civil rights movement, and the feminist movement, changed this, and legislation also backed up these changes. When I took my first academic job in New York in the mid-1960s the Department Chair was a woman, and when I took my first job in US industry in 1985 my boss was a woman. The gender balance changed, but slowly. In the UK companies were very slow to hire women into positions that led to executive roles; in some companies before the mid 1970s women were *only* hired as technicians or secretaries.

As I've said, the manifestation of gender and racial discrimination can be subtle. One of the practices we had in BP in the 1980s was to talk to staff about their 'ultimate potential'. As part of the appraisal process, the manager was to indicate to individuals how far he (almost always he) thought they could progress. Of course this was a very important signal, usually given by someone not competent or skilled enough to give the signal.

The point of raising ultimate potential here is that in

1990 our HR manager, Lyn Richards, had a quick look at the ultimate potentials of male and female employees at the Research Centre. There was a very clear difference between men and women, and I probably don't need to say it was the men who were seen as progressing to higher grades.

When she presented this to the (all male) executive committee, there were loads of suggestions as to how this difference could have occurred, and she was sent back to analyse lots of other factors. And what happened? After every factor was taken into account it became clear that the only reason that could explain the difference was that male team leaders invariably did not see women achieving leadership roles. Once you build something like this into the HR processes of the corporation, it is pretty easy to predict the result. But unless you are scrupulous in examining and testing your processes for this sort of bias you will find it hard to achieve any meaningful sort of diversity goals.

Shortly after I took over as head of the Products Division at BP, one of our junior scientists, of Indian heritage, sent a complaint to the Chairman of the company, alleging that he had been subject to racial abuse over a sustained period of time. He documented this complaint thoroughly. My first response to this was that it was unlikely, perhaps he was too sensitive, after all in a technology centre people valued brains rather than race, and if he was doing a good job he was almost certainly getting treated properly. On the other hand, if his performance was substandard he might just be getting the feedback he needed to improve. I couldn't have been more wrong.

Over several weeks, together with a senior colleague

from HR, we investigated these charges, and what we found was a culture where racial epithets were commonly used in criticising work, where racist cartoons were placed on his desk, and where he was not given the same access to key clients as white counterparts. Even in talking with us during the investigation, managers and team members made racist remarks without being conscious of what they were saying. So there was a deep disease in this team, which we dealt with, but only because one young man spoke out about it.

What can we do to address this? From my experiences I came to feel that new team leaders, as part of training for their first management role, needed to spend some time really getting to grips with these issues. To do this, Dorothy Griffiths of Imperial College and I constructed some short scenarios for discussion at the training course for new team leaders, trying to show that bad behaviour can be very 'in your face' or it can be much more subtle. This is just one sort of training tool, but it certainly generated some very heated discussion among the course participants, and, I think, served to raise awareness by several notches. At the same time, it is necessary in first level manager training to make the company policy very, very clear, and the consequences of not following it equally clear.

There is also much to be done at the highest levels of the company. When BP merged with Amoco, it soon became clear that Amoco had a much stronger policy of advancing women into positions of responsibility than did BP. Doug Ford, who led the downstream business after the merger, made a real difference in appointments that took place while he was there. And not just giving women key jobs, but always recognising that talented people could be pushed harder. So Jeanne Johns, who was, at that time, running BP's Toledo Refinery, was clearly a person with strong commercial skills, and he pushed her to take on a lead role in improving commerciality at the Texas City Refinery. One or two people, in the leadership team of a corporation, can make a big difference.

I recall once discussing women in leadership roles with David Sainsbury, when he was running the supermarket chain in the UK. He told me that he had a list in his desk of the 10 or 20 women most important, and of greatest potential importance, to the corporation. If any of them were to leave, or even think about leaving, he had to be notified of this personally, so that he could speak to them. By having this list, he could also think about their careers as key jobs became vacant. Simple? Sure, but effective things almost always are.

FOR THE WEEKEND:

Jury Service

Living in New York City jury service (or jury duty as it is called in the US) is a regular summons, though in the UK it is less usual to be called. There is a lot of crime, and a lot of civil cases are tried by juries as well. The Zagat guide to New York has a separate section on best places for lunch when on jury duty.

Most executives find as many reasons as possible to postpone this or to not serve. This is a mistake. It is a mistake because we have certain civic duties, and this is one of them. But it is, as well, a chance to learn about aspects of decision making, and short term team building, that you are unlikely to be able to get from any course. Sure, most business teams are established for the long term, but we often have a particular problem to solve, or a deal that is going to get done, that requires bringing together a diverse group for a week of intensive work as a team. That is what a jury has to do.

We make decisions in business all the time. As you become more senior in the corporation, the people with whom you collaborate on decisions are closer and closer to being your peers. This is distinct from some front line management jobs, or leadership roles in the factory, where decisions need to involve everyone from labourers to supervisors. Still, even in those situations, the leader makes the decision and is accountable for it, the others suggest. In the jury room, this is very different. Everyone has to be in on the decision, and be willing to stand up to say, 'Yes, I agree, and I support this verdict.' How a group of people from across the adult population – doctors, maintenance workers, teachers – can come together and learn to do this in a few days, sometimes in a few hours, is quite instructive. And these decisions have big consequences – they can be a matter of life or death.

I received such a summons for jury duty in July 1975, and it referred to events that had occurred about 18 months earlier.

One winter evening in 1973, Rafael, Ricardo and a third man whose identity has not been revealed other than to the police, arrived at the basement apartment of Marta and Dano in the Williamsburg section of Brooklyn. Marta and Dano were at home with their two children, Larita and Carlos, aged one and three. Larita was Dano and Marta's child, and Carlos was the child of Marta and Ricardo.

While Marta and Ricardo had been lovers for several years, and fellow members of a Coney Island gang, they were now not on good terms. Marta had left the gang and was with Dano, who belonged to a rival Hispanic gang centred in Williamsburg.

Ricardo and his two friends forced their way in to the apartment. An argument began immediately. Ricardo demanded that he be allowed to take Carlos to live with him; Marta flatly refused. At some point guns were produced (but it is disputed whether they were already in the apartment or Ricardo brought them) and a scuffle occurred involving all five adults present. When the police arrived, called by neighbours who had heard the sound of shots being fired and people screaming, Rafael and Ricardo were dead. Both had been shot in the crotch and their genitals completely blown to pieces. The cause of death was loss of blood. Marta and Dano were arrested, and both were charged with the double murder. Additional charges relating to weapons were also filed.

The case came to trial in July 1975. More than 100 potential jurors were sworn (to answer all questions truthfully and to the best of their ability, and if selected to serve on the jury as instructed by the Court) to be questioned in groups of 12 by the defence and prosecution, before Judge David Collins. A second group of 75 was required before all twelve jurors and two alternates were seated.

At one point Marta's defence attorney asked a group of potential jurors: 'I may not call my client to testify in her own defence. Would this prejudice you against her?' Ira Levine, a Professor of Chemistry at Brooklyn College, immediately raised his hand to say, 'Yes, I would hold it against her if she didn't testify in her own defence.' At this point Judge Collins leaned forward and said to Dr Levine, 'I will instruct you that you may not hold this against her. It is for the prosecution to prove that she is guilty, and she is not required to testify or do anything else in her own defence.' To which Ira replied, 'I don't care, I would hold it against her anyway.' 'But I just told you that I am instructing you that you may not hold it against her.' 'Look, you made me take an oath to answer all questions put to me truthfully. Then he (the defence attorney) asks me a question and I answer it truthfully, and now you are telling me that I may not give that answer.' Judge Collins leaned back, smiled a wry little smile, and the defence duly excused Professor Levine from the case. Mission accomplished.

How often do we ask our colleagues, subordinates, children, to give us a truthful answer, not wanting to hear the answer they give, even worse, telling them that their truth is not an acceptable truth?

Three jurors had been seated by the time I was called. I gave my profession as scientist, Professor of Chemistry. The defence attorney for Dano suggested to me that as a professional person, PhD and such, I might think my opinion in the jury room deliberations was more important than that of less educated people. 'Would I be able to listen to the views of others and give them equal consideration?' I assured him that I would, but I am not sure that I believed that myself. In any case, I was seated as juror number four. It took most of a day for all twelve jurors, plus two alternates, to be selected. By that time more than 150 had been rejected by one side or the other, or excused by the judge on the basis that because the trial might last as long as two weeks it would be a hardship for them.

The early stages of testimony by witnesses for the prosecution set the scene, and laid out basic facts about Marta, her children, the gang memberships, that were not in dispute. Eventually, through testimony of experts, the prosecution sought to establish that the slayings had been executions, that is, the intruders were lined up against the wall and shot, at least one with a weapon that might have already been in the apartment.

The testimony of witnesses for the defence was much more complicated. Several of them were members of the gang of the dead men, and were asked to testify about practices of rape and murder which the gang practised in Coney Island. Judge Collins did not allow this testimony, and appointed additional lawyers for these witnesses to prevent them from self-incrimination. So in a Brooklyn courtroom these negative character witnesses 'took the fifth', on advice of counsel. All of this was conducted with questions asked in English, through a translator, and answers translated back from Spanish into English. Despite the refusal of the witnesses to self-incriminate, we jurors were left with a clear understanding that raping and murdering were acts required for advancement in the gang hierarchy.

The testimony lasted for 10 days. On day 8, juror number 9 spoke to the judge about a problem he had at work which required his urgent attention. The judge heard this appeal in private with the prosecution and defence attorneys, and with their agreement discharged juror number 9 and replaced him with one of the two alternates. This left the final alternate, a retired custodian of a Brooklyn apartment building, rather lonely, as we were not permitted to speak to him, he did not come into the jury room with us, but stayed in a separate room during the numerous breaks which occurred in the ensuing testimony.

The thrust of the defence case that was laid out before us was that the two men had come to kidnap one or both of Marta's children, at least the older one. That these gang members were encouraged to rape women and gained status in the gang for doing this. That they regularly murdered, and had brought weapons with them for that purpose.

During the entire trial, we jurors were not permitted to take any notes, and no writing equipment was permitted in the jury room. We were not allowed to ask any questions, other than about matters relating to our own schedules and comforts. Throughout, the judge treated the jurors with the utmost courtesy, always apologizing when there were long delays, usually occasioned by differences between the lawyers about admissibility of evidence, which the judge heard outside the presence of the jury. At every break in the proceedings, for lunch, at the end of each day, the judge cautioned the jurors not to discuss the case with each other or with anyone else, including close family members.

A crucial bit of testimony (or so it seemed to me) occurred on day 6. The medical expert who examined the bodies of the victims brought photos which were passed around the jurors. The defence established, convincingly to me, that it was the view of this expert that the shots that killed the two were fired from 6–12 inches away from their bodies. Under cross examination, the prosecution was unable to shake him from this view.

All testimony was completed at the end of day 9, as well as the final statements by the lawyers. On the morning of day 10 Judge Collins addressed the jurors. He started by explaining the need for proof beyond a reasonable doubt. He then moved to a discussion of circumstantial evidence, and when we could accept it as a consideration of innocence or guilt

Then Judge Collins moved to the question of the various charges. There were more and less severe murder and manslaughter charges, and he explained what each required as proof. He indicated to us that if we acquitted the defendants of these charges, there was no need to consider the weapons charges, but if we found them guilty, then they would also be guilty of the weapons charges.

Finally, he moved to a discussion of the law in New York State regarding what constitutes self-defence. A person, he told us, may use 'deadly physical force' in his own defence if he, or someone in his presence, is in danger of being raped, kidnapped, or murdered. Such an event does not actually have to occur, merely that a reasonable person in the same situation would come to this conclusion. Moreover, Judge Collins told us, if you are in a public place and a confrontation involving one of these threats occurs, if there is an opportunity to withdraw you must withdraw, but in your own home you are under no such obligation. So only after all the evidence was presented, and at the very end of the judge's charge to the jury, did we hear this crucial bit of law, the organising principle according to which we had to assess the evidence.

Do we sometimes do this in our own meetings, in the lead up to decisions? Do we keep back the key point until the last, perhaps to increase its impact or because we see it as a way of increasing our own impact on the group?

The jury, having heard this charge from the judge, was instructed to retire to consider the verdict, which had to be unanimous. We would deliberate until we reached a unanimous verdict or agreed that it was impossible to do so. If we needed to review any of the evidence, the foreman (juror number 1) would send a request to the judge, we would be brought back into the courtroom, and the testimony we required would be read back to us by the court stenographer. Likewise, if we were confused or disagreed about anything the judge had told us, we were to send a written question to him and he would explain it to us.

While up to this point we had returned home every evening after the testimony ended, we were told that if we were still deliberating at 10 pm that evening, we would be taken to a hotel, and return in the morning to continue. With that final bit of information, we went to the jury room and were served sandwiches for our lunch. At the judge's option, the alternate juror was not dismissed at this point, but was sent back to the room where he waited alone.

I had, several times in the course of the trial, had lunch with Martin, a psychologist, and juror number 11. As we went to the jury room and everyone milled about, he asked me quietly what I thought. I said, to my way of thinking, they were not guilty, based on the prosecution version of an execution not being supported by the medical evidence, and all three grounds of self-defence being reasonably argued. He agreed, but said, 'I think some of them will feel they have to be guilty of something, after all, they killed two people.'

We began to review the evidence. Later, reflecting on the hours spent doing this, I realised how different our lives and experiences were in this regard. I was an academic scientist and Department Chair at the time, and about to become a University Dean. I spent a lot of my time in meetings and seminars where, for example, other scientists presented their work, or fellow Chairs presented the case for a budget or personnel decision. In a one hour scientific seminar, there are usually 1–3 key points about what the speaker has done that are significant, but rarely does the speaker say: These are the messages I want you to take away from this talk. It happens more often in industry, but not nearly enough. The rest of the hour is filled with two things: data to support that 'what we concluded is substantiated' and 'unfruitful directions we went down before our brilliance led us to this conclusion'. All of the latter can be discarded, and most of the former in figuring out what to take away from the seminar.

So it was with our nine days of courtroom presentations. There were two or three things, taking up in total maybe one hour of the nine days in their presentation that I thought were relevant to the question of innocence or guilt. The medical evidence that supported the defence contention that the shots were fired at close range during a scuffle, rather than the prosecution view that this was an execution; the credibility of the (in part) circumstantial evidence that those in the apartment were in danger of being murdered, kidnapped, or raped. But few in the jury room had been listening in that way, so we spent hours going over matters that were largely inconsequential, but were occupying the thoughts of some of the jurors.

The charge from the judge also inspired a lot of debate. Three times we had questions on which jurors disagreed, leading the foreman to send a note to the judge, who called us back into the courtroom to explain the point in question.

Eventually, from a position where many were undecided, by 6 pm we had moved to 10 of the jurors being in favour of acquittal, one, Juror 3, thinking they should be convicted on a lesser charge than murder, and one, Juror 8, a retired high school teacher, convinced that they were guilty. We were taken across the street from the courthouse to a restaurant for a one hour dinner break. As we sat and ate, the lone alternate had his dinner at a separate table. Some of us looked over and smiled at him.

When we returned from dinner the 10 in favour of acquittal were firm in their positions. Juror 3 was wavering towards acquittal, but Juror 8 wanted to have us re-enact the crime scene, taking up positions and using a broom, that he had found in the closet, as the gun. When all demurred from this activity, he began to do it himself.

At 8:30 pm the police from the court came into our room and announced that they would need the names and phone numbers of our families, given that if we did not reach a verdict in the next 90 minutes we would be sent to a hotel for the night. We can assume that the judge was very familiar with juror behaviour, and knew that sending in these officers might catalyse a decision. So it proved, but in an unexpected way.

No sooner had they left the room than Juror 3 announced that she was happy to go along with the majority, if we thought they were innocent it was ok with her. We cautioned her that she had to be sure of this, that if the judge or the prosecution asked if that was our unanimous verdict she could not show any doubt. She agreed that that was her position. Nothing had changed her mind, except the thought of sleeping in a strange bed being more important than maintaining her view.

We turned to Juror 8, who was now quite distressed. He tried arguing with us again, but got no sympathy, indeed little attention to the points he was trying to make. At 8:55 pm he asked the foreman to send a note to the judge on his behalf. The note read 'Juror number 8 has become ill. He regurgitated his dinner and is feeling very bad, and wants to be excused.' The Judge, on receiving this note, called Juror 8 into the court. About 10 minutes later we were all called to the courtroom. Judge Collins told us that in view of the illness of Juror 8 he had excused him from further service, and the alternate would take his place. We were to return to the jury room with the alternate and see if we could agree a verdict.

When we came into the jury room there was a bit of commotion. Martin and I looked at each other, then Martin turned, smiled at our new juror, and said, 'Look, we are all agreed on the verdict, but the fellow who you replaced disagreed with us. We can go through everything again with you, but perhaps it would be simplest if we didn't tell you what we were agreed on, but asked how you would vote regarding the charges.'

The new juror looked around at us, and said, 'I would vote for them being not guilty on all charges.' Everyone breathed out then. The foreman said, 'Should we stay here for half an hour so it doesn't look like what just happened happened?' She got no votes for that process. In a minute she called the officer and handed him a note saying that we had reached a unanimous verdict.

When we filed back into the courtroom, the lawyers and defendants looked at us, searching for a clue as to what we had decided. I could not resist. I looked at Marta and smiled, then we took our seats and the verdict was read out.

The judge thanked us very much for our service, told us how important it was that we did this, and sent us home with the gratitude of the court. I agreed; we had done something worthwhile together.

SPRING

'*Blossom by blossom the spring begins*'

Swinburne

WEEK 13

The Great Outdoors

I don't know who originated the fad for taking middle and upper managers, or candidates for such posts, out of the office and into the woods for a week, but it has been very popular for quite a while now. Extreme versions of this have been the subject of several dramatic television documentaries, and may have inspired some of the survival-type reality TV shows.

Like many people, I was a big critic of outdoors-y courses without ever having experienced one. I felt that they were artificial, unnecessarily stressful for individuals, possibly discriminatory in a way that was inconsistent with the qualities we seek in assessing the potential for success, and poor learning environments.

Some of these criticisms are valid. More than other courses there is a real potential for doing damage to individuals (and I don't just mean physical injury, though that too) on these courses. Sure, you can do some harm in a classroom setting, but mostly the bad courses in classrooms just bore participants.

Still, through my participation in such programmes, I have become convinced that a well-designed programme that takes people away from their normal work environment into completely artificial situations can be very valuable. But these programmes have to be thought through very carefully, run by very skilled and experienced individuals, and you have to be prepared to spend a lot of money on the course. So this is *not* about sending 12 people up a river with four canoes and seeing who comes back. It is about designing an environment for learning, self-awareness, and feedback. Ideally it also forms close bonds between participants which carry over into the support they give one another in running a corporation. And it should be fun, at least some of the time.

The first outdoor course I experienced was designed for people who already held quite senior positions in the company. Probably the organisers felt that they were developing in us aspects of senior peer team behaviour and cooperation, looking at strategic thinking in situations of stress, and ability to deal with problems of greater and greater abstraction. And it did do all of this. But the most important thing this course did for me was to provide a mirror of my own behaviour in the situations which were created. There is nothing as valuable to a senior executive as non-judgemental, descriptive feedback, yet there are so few opportunities to get this feedback in corporate life.

The outdoor course was a week-long exploration of problems. It was set in a lakefront hotel, which we took over

completely for a week, in the winter, for just a dozen participants. The course started with problems that were complex, but for which it was clear at the outset how to reach
the solution. Certain bits of data needed to be accumulated
(this involved using maps and compasses to pilot a canoe
to points on the lake, in the dark), the data needed to be
assembled, equations developed and solved, and the results
used to solve the problem. So a known problem, known
solution, but one which still had to be solved by working
together.

When you have people of equivalent seniority participating in such a course, with no one put in charge by a
company-sanctioned hierarchy, you test competencies that
are important for senior teams in many real life situations
in companies. And all of us need to ask ourselves, how do I
contribute to the solution, am I behaving as a team member
(when I am used to being the leader), how well do I know
my own strengths and weaknesses so I can assume the role
which maximises my contribution? These are important
questions for self-examination and they are important for
how individuals will function at the most senior level in a
corporation.

The course then moved on to problems in which we
knew what the problem was, we knew that there was a way
of solving the problem, but we had to work out, through
our own learning and actions, how to find that solution. So
a more complex type of problem, and one we encounter all
the time in business.

Here I want to bring out another important feature
of the course. In working through the problem, we found

ourselves stuck in a particularly nasty mess regarding strategy, its communication, and its implementation. When this happened, the organisers were able to just call a time-out, and we could sit in a room and say 'Now look at this mess we are in. Isn't this just the exact situation in which we often find ourselves? So let's take the luxury of being on the course instead of being in our offices, to think about how we got here, and how we get ourselves out of this mess.' This is a great opportunity for learning (and one which I also discuss in Week 45. The Leader as Teacher).

Finally, we tackled problems of the most difficult kind, the kind that occur in business and ultimately determine which companies succeed against their competitors. These are the situations where we don't know what the problem is, or even if there is one. There are only events, and from these events we must consider how to act most effectively in the interests of our company. How do we organise ourselves to respond to what is happening, how do we sort out red herrings from matters of import, when do we take bold action, when do we wait a bit to see how things unfold? And if we have waited too long, how do we recover our position? This is the real world made artificial, contained but still very involving. I don't think anyone in these situations was able to step back and behave as if it was a game rather than something that commanded their full attention.

How did I learn about my own behaviour on this sort of course? In part, because there were a number of very skilled psychologists present throughout, taking frequent time-outs with me as an individual and in small groups to talk over what had just happened, my reactions and learning. Those professionals quickly developed our confidence to talk to them privately about interactions, performance, and concerns for others.

That is during the course. But throughout the week, video recording of the proceedings took place, with staff members wandering through all the different activities. It is amazing how oblivious to this we become after a while.

At one point in this particular week, I was approached by three of the participants who had become very upset about the behaviour of one of the others who was a close colleague of mine back at work. 'Listen, you're his friend, so sit down with him and talk to him about this, because otherwise we think it would be best if he took a walk in the mountains and didn't come back for a few days.'

It is not an easy thing, having a heart to heart talk with someone you know well, but have to go back to work with the following week. Still, after I had spent about an hour thinking about how to do it, I sat down in a room with Mike and we talked. Intensively. Later, one of the course staff said to me, 'Wait until you see the recording of your discussion with Mike' and I said, 'How could there be a recording, only the two of us were in the room?' 'No, I was there sitting on the sofa the whole time' was his reply. We were so completely absorbed in the conversation that neither of us had the slightest idea we were being recorded.

About a month after the course ended, I got a video in the mail. About an hour long, it had been excerpted from the extensive recording that had been done during the week to show me in different situations. With no one else present, I took this into a small room and played it, watching myself, seeing what I liked and what I hated about my own behaviour as the camera caught it. Descriptive, non-judgemental feedback. We all need it, and we need to have our minds open to learn from it.

WEEK 14

Cultural and Moral Relativism

A company that operates globally faces some difficult challenges when it comes to deciding what it will and will not do. It seems easy enough, sitting in a US or EU headquarters building, to make statements like 'We hold the same environmental standards for our operations wherever we operate in the world' or 'Our company supports the principles set forth in the UN Universal Declaration of Human Rights', but how do these statements translate into actions in Africa, the Middle East, rural China, Russia, and lots of other places?

Environmental issues are widely discussed. What about the social issues? How difficult is this? Well, a quick reading of the UN Universal Declaration of Human Rights gives you a pretty good idea of how difficult. For example, Article 21 states:

'The will of the people shall be the basis of the
authority of government; this will shall be expressed
in periodic and genuine elections which shall be by
universal and equal suffrage and shall be held by
secret vote or by equivalent free voting procedures.'

Now, how many multinational companies are operating in
countries where this is not true, while simultaneously saying on the websites that they are supporting the principles
of the UN Declaration of Human Rights?
And what about Article 16?

'(1) Men and women of full age, without any
limitation due to race, nationality or religion, have
the right to marry and to found a family. They
are entitled to equal rights as to marriage, during
marriage and at its dissolution.

(2) Marriage shall be entered into only with the free
and full consent of the intending spouses.'

Well, this is a challenge to some of the countries many
of us work in. And in case you haven't looked at it for a
while, there are 30 articles along these lines, and a meaty
preamble as well. But then again, we can't really imagine
the counterfactual of any US or EU company stating as its
policy 'We **do not** support the UN Universal Declaration on
Human Rights', now, can we?

So there are some tough problems which basically
come down to issues of culture and morals. Wherever

we operate, we need to be sensitive to cultural differences. These differences often manifest themselves in the roles of men and women in societies. In seemingly trivial things like whether to shake hands, when to talk on the phone in the presence of others, or even when to not blow your nose. There are also cultural differences, vast ones, in how business or government regulation is done. What constitutes a political contribution, what is an appropriate level of entertainment to offer to a Government official, or what it is appropriate to accept.

But while we behave in a culturally sensitive way, we must always have in mind our morality. A company must know what behaviour violates its moral codes, and would be unacceptable wherever it was practised. In other words, we can accept and work across a wide cultural relativism, but we have no space for moral relativism.

Does this get us out of the dilemma I posed about the UN Universal Declaration on Human Rights? I think it can, if you reason along these lines:

The UN Declaration is not a statement of how the world is today, but a set of goals of how you want it to be. So your support of it is a statement that your company not only supports the goals, but in its business is working towards achieving them.

This is an important statement – because it says that as a global corporation you have goals other than just making money this quarter. Your business in a country is for the long term, and in the long term that business will survive and prosper under conditions where human rights are respected.

Now what do we mean by 'working towards achieving it'? Well, it means that you believe that you can be a **force for good** in the country. And this is not just about contributing to the local museum or building a school, however much those both might be good things to do. It means that you can convince yourself that money derived from your business that stays in the country, and in particular with the government of the country, is leading to the human rights goals you support.

Making decisions about this is always difficult. How does a company decide that it is possible to be a force for good in Angola but not Sudan? Only by thinking through the systems in place, or that can be put in place, and en- suring that they work in line with our expectations. It takes tough minded people, both in the corporate centre and in the countries where the corporation operates, people who are able to build relationships that allow for the sort of communication on these issues that leads to change.

So in global corporations, one is always being sensitive to cultural differences, but the leadership and all its execu- tives must also know their moral code. As a result, they know where there is a line that cannot be crossed. Cultural relativism is not only acceptable, it is an important part of working in the global corporation. Moral relativism is not only unacceptable, its unacceptability is a crucial part of the work of a global corporation and making clear what the company stands for.

WEEK 15

Help: Getting Advice from the Dreaded Consultants

In a well-run company, central corporate groups are kept lean, especially in areas on which these are only occasional demands. There is no point in having endless strategy groups as standing entities if strategy is only really reviewed and worked on from time to time. But if this is the case, as new initiatives arise, or questions are raised about whether to continue an ongoing activity, how do we find the resources to answer these questions?

The answer is: consultants. And there is probably nothing that arouses as much passion among corporate leadership as the subject of consultants and their value. Too many of us have been subjected to the effects of a large team of consultants coming in to review a broad swathe of the company, with resulting chaos and turmoil. Sometimes it works out, but most of the time it doesn't.

But the McKinseys, Booz Allens, BCGs and their brethren of the consulting world have a function, and a very useful one at that. They help us expand the workforce, bring new ideas to a problem (often new to us, not to them), and mobilise reserves of data and information that are difficult to access.

So if you are asking a person in the company to look at the intellectual property strategy, or the procurement strategy, or whether you should be operating in South Africa, or what the opportunities might be in the pulp and paper industry – whatever the challenge, let's get that person some help. Help not just in the form of a small temporary team to tackle the problem (which may be necessary), but help also in the form of consultants who can make the project live.

I learned this lesson the hard way, by trying to do everything myself (showing how much money I could save, as well as how smart I was) with a very small team, trying to tackle a big problem. I got something done, but it was not at the level of professionalism that my management had a right to expect. With a little outside help I could have turned some good ideas into a really good strategic project.

As we all know, consultancy firms, even the biggest and most competent, are not uniformly capable. They have strengths and you have to select so as to play to those strengths. Indeed, what we are sometimes trying to do is be the fourth or fifth client of the firm in a particular area, so we get the benefit of all the accumulated information and thinking. But we also want innovative thinking, and, above all, responsiveness to the challenge we are facing.

Consultants must not be encouraged to parrot back to

us our prejudices. If they do then they are not earning their keep. Nor must they recycle some stuff from their files that is only marginally relevant. The best will never do this, but the second and third best will do so frequently.

Even working with the best consulting firms, success requires a lot of effort on your part as well as theirs. You have to be there to interact with them, to be sure that their style of presentation suits your own company culture, and to be certain that what they are telling you is well grounded in evidence. After all, in the end you are not going to present this to your management as the McKinsey report, but as work that you are willing to stand for yourself.

As the employer of the consulting firm, you need to be very clear about who is actually going to be working on the project. It is a favourite trick to trot out the very sharp consultant when they are trying to win the business, replacing that person with someone at a much lower level of competence when the work is actually going to be done.

Substantial engagements with a single consulting firm gives you a lot of leverage over who works with you, and a lot of knowledge about who is really able to deliver on a particular kind of project. But that does not say that any one firm is best for all sorts of jobs. I think that many of us find that some are really good on strategic problems but not much use on driving operational excellence, and vice versa. Some are very good on organisation, others on technical matters. These big consulting firms develop personalities, strengths, and weaknesses. They go through periods of increasing capability and periods of decline. So to really get the best value for your money you need to know a fair amount about them. That up front effort will pay off in the product you get.

One characteristic of many of these firms is that they develop a particular language – yes, it is English but with phrases or ways of expressing things that are peculiar to them. This is some of their intellectual property. In most consulting engagements it is innocent enough, and you may even find it useful. But there is one danger zone. Consultants can be very useful on getting groups to be highly productive, to find new ways of looking at problems to produce extraordinary results. But I have often found that those consultants are particularly adept at getting the team with whom they are working to adopt a new language as part of the breakthrough process. This is all to the good, until the team members start to interact with other people in the company who have not been through the same training, using phrases like 'the background conversation I am having is . . .' while the others look at them in puzzlement. It is up to the leadership to keep this in check, because the interest of the consulting firm is to say that you can solve this problem by putting all your employees through our training programme!

Finally, a well-run selection process will pay big dividends. To run a process (rather than just call McKinsey!) you need to think through the brief in some detail with the internal team. Written responses from a half dozen firms will give you an idea of how they will approach the problem, and some of these ideas, even from those you don't select, will be valuable additions to your own thinking. After that, a one-hour meeting with each of a shortlist of three will help you understand whether you can work with the firm, do the people you are going to be working with have an in-depth understanding of the written materials they sent you (or were they written by someone else), and most important, will these guys challenge us to produce a high quality product?

WEEK 16

Peer Groups

In any big, geographically diverse, company, there are groups of business leaders at the same level, running similar operations in different parts of the world. Even in companies operating in a single relatively large country, there are such groups. They could be the leaders who run retail operations organised by country or region, or those who run manufacturing plants making similar products. In companies where discovery plays a big role, such as Oil Exploration or Drug Discovery, big companies will usually have leaders accountable for making these 'discoveries' in different places (geographic) or business sectors.

One challenge for the senior leadership of any company is how much power to give to these groups of peers for resource allocation in their activity space. With this goes the corresponding question of accountability of the peer group for performance of the whole activity.

The traditional approach to management views giving

resources and accountability to groups such as these as anathema. First, the dogma would go that the group cannot necessarily have enough insight into corporate strategy to align resources with that strategy. Second, theory says that shared accountability is always a bad idea, and that accountability must always rest with a single person.

Let's put aside theory and dogma for a second, and ask ourselves some bigger example questions: How do I get the best economic outcome from my collection of sixteen factories around the world? How do I best decide where in the world I should introduce new retail practices first? How do I allocate my scarce capital budget among exploration or drug discovery plays in different parts of the world? How do I best budget for and derive value from a big R and D programme in support of a business area?

Probably transcending all of these questions is the potential for motivation of the leaders comprising a peer group. Because in my experience, pushing down accountability to groups like these is tremendously motivating. And beyond the possibility of really good decision-making implied by the questions above, the value of a group of peers, driven to show how much they can contribute to the corporation, is incalculable.

I saw this value in BP in different peer groups over time. In Exploration, where the practice started, the exploration managers from around the world took on the collective accountability for finding as much oil as they could within the constraints of an annual expenditure. It was a sizeable amount of money, $400 million per year if I recall. They replaced a process whereby each one bid into the centre of the business for his share of the pie, with a collective process in which the goal was completely different – getting the biggest bang for the total bucks spent. The discussions and mutual challenge associated with coming up with such a plan, carried out by regional managers and technical experts sitting in a room, gave a better result than the system it replaced.

In Refining, there is also the issue of allocating capital, to both upgrade refineries and supply new markets, for example a booming aviation fuel market in north eastern Australia, or a clean diesel market in Europe. But the refinery managers, a small central team supporting them, and the technology leadership that they funded, also looked hard at how their performance was measured. Refining needed to improve its return on capital employed. Before the creation of the peer group, each refinery or regional grouping of refineries pushed to get as big a capital budget as it could, because, after all, they had so many good ideas of things to do. When the peer group worked on this, they came out with a different approach: essentially they said, 'We want to make as much money as possible with as little capital expenditure as we can. That's the way we get our returns up.' They set the right goal for themselves, and were motivated by it, rather than having the corporate centre set it for them.

But refineries – indeed all factories – are about much more than allocating capital. They are about running the equipment to very high levels of availability. They are about commerciality, in both how they acquire their feedstock and how they get their products into the market.

And staffing levels, and energy costs, and maintenance, and trying out new technologies for production and control. The peer group tackled lots of these things. They were able to decide to collectively fund development of a new technology or system, trial it in one place, evaluate the results, and then implement it across the world. They served a human resources development function as well, building experience by moving people around the world, grooming their own successors, and spreading good practices.

In BP-speak, what the peer groups had was space, space that was reserved for the centre before the peer group was created. Space in which to enhance performance by working together, taking accountability for delivering that performance. To make this work, the centre had to give up something to the peer group, and this was not easy to do, especially at the beginning. Some members of the central executive wanted to be present at the peer group and participate in all its meetings. They had to learn that they were not peers, and their presence there changed the entire process. Even a more limited involvement, like the senior executive coming in at the end of a peer group meeting to hear a report on what they had accomplished over a two- or three-day meeting, is, in my view, a bad idea. Inevitably in that situation a part of the valuable meeting time becomes dedicated to preparing the report to the executive who will turn up at the end.

More useful is for an executive to turn up at the beginning, to share context of where the business is, pressures on performance, new strategic directions, corporate priorities, etc. Share the context, then disappear and let these guys get on with their work. Or come by one evening for drinks and dinner and share things then. In either case, be open and frank; treat these peer groups as grown-ups who you are counting on to deliver big things for the company.

But space is bounded. So peer groups have to understand both the space that they have and the boundaries. And making that clear is also the responsibility of the senior executive. Space and boundaries both have to be maintained; changes, and the rationale for these changes, have to be clearly communicated.

When peer groups work well, they are much more than networks that meet occasionally to share ideas. The members are always there to support each other to deliver the collective goal. One of the most moving moments of my business career came at the end of a three-day meeting of the Global Refining Network (GRN), the peer group of the refiners. As we were closing the meeting, and using our process of having everyone say their piece about what we had and had not accomplished, one of the refinery managers said, 'Look, this meeting is over, but that doesn't mean that we now go our separate ways until the next meeting. As far as I'm concerned, the GRN is always in session.' When a tough refinery manager says something like that, you just want to get up and have a group hug!

WEEK 17

Ethics and the Corporation

Bill O'Brien, who spent many years working as a senior executive in the insurance industry, often spoke about ethics and values in companies. One of his lovely examples was of a company that boasts in its annual report about the increases in sales it has seen in the year just completed, while haranguing employees inside the company because 'the competition has been increasing sales so much faster than we are'. And of course the employees think: If they are willing to lie to the shareholders about this, what other lies might they be telling us?

The leadership of a company sets an ethical tone that pervades everything that employees in the company do. When management refuses to enter into a business transaction because they do not believe it is within the ethical standards of the corporation, it can assume that everyone in the company, not just the people in the meeting, knows about this decision. Decisions like these become a factor in what individuals do and propose to do.

Enron is the 'negative role model' for this. We might ask, why if Enron created an apparently attractive business model other oil and gas companies didn't follow the new model. After all, the Enron share price performance, for several years, left other oil companies far behind. The reason is a difference of view of business ethics.

I was at a short course for senior BP managers at Harvard Business School in early 2000, just before Enron's problems started to emerge in the press, where the faculty devoted a morning to Enron, the theme being 'Why can't BP be more like Enron? These guys have invented a new way of doing business, and you are still living in the past.' There was lots of discussion, including BP Trading leadership pointing out that we actually made more money trading than Enron did, but the defining moment for me came when someone from BP said: ' Look, we hear what you say, but we just cannot do the things that Enron does. We have certain ethical principles about how we run our business, and they don't allow us to do what those guys are doing. Maybe what they are doing is legal, that is not the point. They just are not consistent with how we do our business.'

Of course the HBS faculty thought we were dinosaurs. But they were wrong about who would become extinct soonest.

By way of contrast:

Struan Robertson, then head of Retail Marketing in BP, once appeared before the quarterly review of the refining and marketing business to present a proposed retail joint venture in Japan, a new geography for BP. He had started into his presentation, showing various aspects of store format, site acquisition, projected sales, etc. when John Browne interrupted him. 'Struan,' he said, 'I believe you have assessed this very well, and that you are a complete professional about marketing, so I don't really need you to prove it with this case. But tell me about our Japanese partner. What does he do? Has he ever been accused of financial irregularities? Are his ethical standards consistent with ours?'

You can be sure that this line of inquiry by the CEO was well known throughout the business by the end of that day.

On ethics, sure it is important to have a policy, and it is necessary to communicate that policy very clearly, both in writing and the training given to front line managers, but actions are what make the policy live. Not the 'easy actions', like making sure that the company does not offer or accept bribes, but the tough ones, where there is a judgement call to be made on a business transaction, and the ethical policy determines how that call is made.

So many of these ethics judgement calls occur in developing countries, and it seems appropriate, especially for large companies, to try to have the structure in a country that has both a business line management and a country line management. By the country line, I mean something like the President of Corporation A in Country X. This person is not the one making the business decisions in country, but does have all the responsibility for relations with the Government. He or she also has the oversight accountability for being sure that the businesses operating in his or her country are doing so in accordance with the global standards for the corporation. So while it may be absolutely common practice for businesses in Country X to have karaoke parties for their customers with prostitutes supplied, it is up to the Country President to say, 'Sorry, but we don't do this, find some other way to entertain them.' And this means that the President's word has to be final on such things, trumping the business unit leader.

If such a structure is not possible, or deemed too expensive, then I think every company operating globally needs to think of other structures, and assurance mechanisms behind these structures, to give itself confidence that its code of ethics is being followed.

There are both Board and executive roles in all this. The Board's job is to ensure that the ethics policies are in place, and represent standards that they as a Board stand behind. The executive must be sure that the business systems are in place to carry out these policies, in such a way that they can provide substantive assurance to the Board on a regular basis. As with many things, but well illustrated here, the Board's role is governance, the executive role is management. But the executive must know (or it will surely find out) that if it does the management role poorly the Board will cross the line into management. When this happens the executive has failed.

FOR THE WEEKEND

Growth of Confidence

The summers when I was 17 and 18 years old I worked at a children's camp run by the New Jersey YM and YWHA (Young Men's and Young Women's Hebrew Association, the Jewish response to the YMCA). The first summer I was a regular 'counselor', taking care of a bunch of 12 year olds. The second summer I talked my way into being the 'pioneering specialist' for the younger kids, teaching them basic camping skills, pitching tents, doing Morse code, tying knots, that sort of stuff. After all, I had been a Boy Scout, and spent four summers at Boy Scout camp. After the summer ended, it was possible to make some additional money by working an extra week taking the whole camp apart for the winter, physical labour but outdoors and with a crew of other friends from the summer.

One night during this post-season work week, we were sitting and talking, around a campfire I recall, and a fellow named Bernie Greenspan, who was an art student, said something memorable: I find that it really helps to have an air of competence. If I want to make some money painting a mural in a shop window, I have to convey to the owner that I am a guy who can do this and it will be beautiful and persuasive.

Until that moment, my attitude had been that it was cooler not to show competence, not to study too hard, or try to be the best. Maybe it made not achieving at a high level easier to take if you weren't trying too hard. I realised then that while I was competent, and seemed competent, in the role I had in camp, when I thought about my home and university life that was not what I projected. And at the root of this, there was a connection between competence and confidence. Pretty obvious, but if you are either timid or frivolous, in my case often the latter to cover up the former, you don't appear competent and confident. But when I came home from that summer I started to try harder, to look and act like the person who could achieve, and I did.

My sister Rena understood this early on as well. When she started her real work career, after college graduation and a year of teaching, she spent a couple of years in Paris. She found work, not easy without much French, and survived. But when she returned to New York she had that air of competence, and got jobs with *The New Yorker*, with Joseph Hirschhorn when he was starting the gallery in Washington, and then with various companies writing travel books. She had no real qualifications for any of the jobs, but when she entered the office for an interview she conveyed a feeling that she was a person you could depend on to do this job, whatever it was.

Of course you need to back up the air of competence with competent action. But perhaps one follows the other. At least in my case they did, and still do.

My emergence from timidity to confidence goes back a few years before the campfire chat described above; indeed it started when I was about 14 years old. I was required, as part of the honours program at Jamaica High School, to take a one-term course in public speaking. It was a pretty easy course to teach – we would have two classes of instruction, and then a month where each of us got up and gave a talk. The first one was 'to inform'. I was so nervous, I practised and practised with my little note cards, and managed to deliver something which was marginally acceptable.

I can't recall what happened next, I think a speech to describe our favourite radio or television programme, and why we liked it. I did a little bit better.

And then we had to do a speech 'to persuade'. I had read an article about the upcoming presidential election arguing that Dwight Eisenhower was too old and too ill to run again, and that there were others who should replace him. I got interested in this, read up on it, and prepared my talk. Something happened to me. I got up and spoke with passion. I didn't even need my note cards. The comments that came back to me from the teacher and other students now changed from my previous 'that was ok' to 'you were terrific'. My mother said to me some years later that she thought that course in public speaking changed me, indeed, that she could see it without even knowing what had happened in the classroom. And she was right. I wasn't the scared kid I had been, I had the beginning of being a confident adult. There was still a lot of work to do, in a sense this work has never ended, but I had taken the first step on the journey.

A requirement of my final year as an undergraduate was to do a senior research thesis. In the previous spring, the university got some money from the National Science Foundation to support undergraduate research in the summer. There was an announcement one morning that the top ten undergraduate chemistry students, by grades, would receive these summer stipends to start their thesis work during the summer. A meeting would be held that afternoon to announce the winners. I actually paid little attention to this, because I didn't think I was in the top ten, and because I already had a summer job working at camp again. My grades had improved, from a rather mediocre beginning, but I was sure there were many others ahead of me.

Early evening that day, my friend Charlie Deber caught up with me. He had been to the meeting, he was clearly a top ten, and told me that I had been awarded one of the summer research fellowships. Apparently I was number 10. I told my parents that evening, and agreed that I had to resign my camp position at once and take this.

I joined the lab of Professor Robert Bauman. Bob Bauman was an assistant professor, a physical chemist who did molecular spectroscopy. It was, in some ways, a strange choice. Bauman was an odd character, and I didn't know him well. He was not a rising star in the profession, nor was he a star that had already risen. Such people existed in the department. He was young, but dressed and acted old.

But there was something about his character, and the area in which he was working, that appealed to me. The Chemistry Department was doing some great physical chemistry, my area of interest – Rudolph Marcus was there still, and Herbert Morawetz did very interesting physical chemistry of polymers. For some reason I didn't speak to either of them, and if I had my scientific life would undoubtedly have taken a very different course.

Bob Bauman proposed the following problem to me. If four carbon atoms are put together in a ring, that ring could either be planar or not planar, i.e. puckered. The difference between the two was one of symmetry, and it should, in principle, be possible to determine the symmetry by seeing how the molecule interacted with infrared radiation. Well, so he said, and so I believed him. It turned out that several people, including Bauman, had looked at this problem before, and about half had concluded that it was certainly planar, and about half that it was definitely puckered. That is how clear and definitive science can be on simple problems.

Although I had had three years of rigorous undergraduate education in chemistry, I had none of the tools required to work on this problem, let alone solve it. So I appeared in the lab one day, first day of summer, and was introduced to the graduate students who worked there, Stan Abramowitz, Mary Caldera, and Jim Considine. They started to teach me the experimental techniques, and gave me books to read so that I could have enough theory to interpret the experiments. And what I realised was that my teachers had given me an essential tool without my knowing it: The ability to learn new things on my own. That is the difference between a second rate undergraduate education and a first rate one: in a second rate university you learn formulas and how to solve specific kinds of problems. In a first rate place you learn how to learn. So that was great. I could read, try things, ask questions, read and learn some more.

But there was another thing I learned about myself. Each week the ten students in this special summer research program got together with our advisor, Professor Ernie Becker, and we had to talk about what we were doing. I loved this. Not only had I learned new things, but I wanted to teach my peers. I was not unique in that – most of my fellow students liked doing it too.

So here are two core competencies, not often discussed: an ability to learn new things, take in a lot of technical information, digest and apply it. And a love of communicating what you have learned to others. These competencies need to be developed in each of us, and will serve you well throughout your career.

Both of these competencies seem to me to require a lot of confidence, and I was fortunate to have the opportunity at age 19 to develop that confidence in the safety of the research lab. But of course I had a foundation to build on, one that started in Public Speaking class at Jamaica High School several years earlier.

In June of 1962, having worked on my project for nearly a year, I had the chance to present my work at an undergraduate research symposium for New York City Chemistry students, run by the American Chemical Society. Students from around the City came, and all ten of us from Poly certainly participated. We made slides, prepared a talk, 15 minutes I think, and travelled out to St John's University to compete with others, for it was a competition. A panel of faculty judged our talks and awarded prizes. I had practised my talk with the graduate students from the lab, and had lots of criticisms from them a week before the big day. I went over it again and again. But when I got up in front of that room full of students and faculty, all nervousness disappeared, and I was fluent. Today, more than 45 years and hundreds of presentations later, I can remember that feeling of playing for an audience, what I imagine an actor must feel in the theatre. I won first prize, a cheque for $100.

WEEK 18

Relationships of Mutual Advantage

John Browne once said that BP should stand for relationships of mutual advantage, characterised by humility. What a profound statement of a company and its values! Wherever we turn in business, as with our personal lives, success is about relationships.

I use this phrase over and over again in trying to build partnerships. Sometimes I use it aloud in a meeting, sometimes I just keep it in my head. When I stick to it rigorously I succeed, and when I forget it, in the rush or arrogance to get things done the way I want them done, failure is assured.

It is easiest to have a relationship of mutual advantage, characterised by humility, with a peer company. If BP works on something with DuPont, there is mutual respect, both companies speak the same business language, have similar ideas about what is important, and the relationship has a good chance of flowing smoothly. Don't get me wrong, there is still a lot of work to do, it is just relatively easier than other relationships.

But when a giant company interacts with a small one, everything can become skewed. Mutual advantage often becomes taking advantage. Staff of the big company feel that learning is one-directional and don't open themselves up to real two-way interaction. They are wrong. There is learning for the big company people, probably in abundance, but because you get used to doing things in a 'big company way', through your established processes, you don't use your eyes to see how smaller companies get things done differently – for example faster because of the necessity for slicker process. Between companies of unequal size, what should be a relationship seeks a different level, and becomes that of a purchaser dealing with a vendor. The driver becomes price not value. Price is important, but it is not the same thing as seeking mutual advantage.

Even more difficult is the relationship between a big company and a venture capital group. Such relationships have become increasingly important to the pharmaceutical and information technology industries. Here there is arrogance present in abundance – or as some would put it, too much testosterone in the room to have a relationship. And what a pity, because there is so much learning possible on both sides. Big companies take time to understand markets, to analyse country risk. They see supply chains in a very integrated way. Big companies have access to large amounts of capital at lower cost, and are (or should be) skilled at managing the deployment of that capital.

Venture capitalists are good at other things. They

analyse situations using very limited resources and often limited information on risk. They make decisions quickly. They nurture, yet they are very goal-focused. One might think that venture capitalists work on ideas when they are at an early stage and big companies only when they are mature. Not true actually. What we find is that big companies often start out work on new ideas in their research programmes, but lack the skills (or patience) to bring these ideas through to where they can make a material impact on the corporation. It is this gap that the venture community fills very well. A real relationship between venture capital and a big corporation can result in a lot of learning and a lot of value. But it rarely happens. Relationships depend on people, and in this case as a leader you need to find people (probably more than one) who are influential in your own, big, company, yet open to learning from their work with the venture community.

Another difficult area for relationships is between companies and universities. In most cases (and this represents hundreds of millions of dollars of spending each year, largely wasted) neither the company nor the university is thinking of it as a relationship. The company may be thinking grant, help for old friends, charity, or cheap labour. The university may be thinking a new source of funding, getting out from under government processes for research money, patents and royalties from applied research. But if one really works at a relationship between company and university so much more is possible.

So how do we make it work? As with the relationships in our personal lives, by investing time; talking and listening, and then doing it some more. Always thinking 'what I am going to give my partner in this relationship that will make him want to give me more?' Mutual advantage. Always recognising that I am doing this because I can learn a lot. Characterised by humility.

When I set up the BP–Princeton relationship, which subsequently also involved Ford, we spent a lot of time talking with the Princeton faculty about the idea that this would be a relationship, not a grant with a report to us once a year. And they talked to us about their needs, and I tried to listen to this as well. But it was only after the contracts had been signed between the two companies and the university that we all sat down for three days to work together on what we would actually do, how we saw the technical problems, and what our processes would be. At the end of those three days Professor Rob Socolow, co-leader of the new research centre, said, 'Now I finally know what you were talking about when you said all that stuff about relationships.'

WEEK 19

Chairing

We have all seen people do a really poor job at chairing a meeting. Nothing could be easier:

- Have no idea what the objective is for an agenda item. Lack familiarity with what is being discussed.

- Ignore people who are trying to be heard.

- Let others speak for too long when everyone else in the room is bored.

- Interrupt speakers to interject your own views at inappropriate moments.

- Let an agenda item end inconclusively, and move on to the next disaster.

Have you seen this happen? Have you done it yourself? Do you have someone who will tell you if you are guilty of these errors?

Here are some of the lessons I learned by observing very skilled meeting chairs:

Be clear about who should and should not be present, but err on the side of generosity. There are some people who may not participate very much but will learn by being in the room. Meetings where you are reviewing progress against objectives of a business or function can be very useful places to convey strategic emphasis and determination to achieve performance levels. Of course there are other meetings in companies where a productive outcome depends on only a small number of people being around a table, expressing their views in front of their peers. This is a judgement the Chair needs to make.

(A similar issue arises with Boards. The Board of a company or charity often needs to have individuals who are not board members come and present a particular agenda item. For most large companies, this is a formal process, and it is unthinkable that the presenters would sit in the Board meeting for other agenda items. But in smaller companies, there is an option for the Chairman to have senior executives, not on the Board but crucial to the success of the company, be present for larger parts, or even the entire Board meeting. They learn, sometimes they are invited to contribute, and the company is strengthened. Again, it is an option and one that requires judgement on the part of the Chair, in consultation with others on the Board.)

Do lots of advance preparation. Be sure that there is a clear answer to what you are hoping to accomplish with each agenda item, and what the process is going to be to reach that goal. Get a sense of whether the time allocated is likely to be sufficient, and, given that this is imperfect, which agenda items are your priorities and which can be dropped. Alternatively, if things do run over time, are the objectives more important than ending the meeting on time? Make sure others understand that while we are going to do our best to finish on time, you are going to allow the meeting to continue for longer than originally planned if necessary.

Advance preparation also means knowing a lot about what is going to be presented, what decisions are going to be asked for, what conflicting views might surface. This doesn't mean that everything has to be scripted in advance, but it does mean that good quality pre-reading must be prepared, and that, as Chairman, you have probed with appropriate staff to understand the issues. As Chair you can ask to see all the slides that will be used ahead of the meeting, ask questions about them, and give yourself enough time to think through the direction you will want the discussion to take. The role of the Chairman requires a time commitment well in excess of the time for the meeting.

Guide towards the place you want to go, but listen to the views of others. There are subtle ways of doing this, and more confrontational. For example, an approach is for the Chair to state the answer and then see if anyone will offer an alternative. This is also a technique to practise, because at its best it shows who is willing to stand up to the boss with a different view, and to defend that view. But be self-aware: if the alternative view never wins people will stop expressing it. In a venture capital group I worked with, the Senior Partner often expressed a view after a presentation, and then everyone else chimed in with a version of 'I agree with Alan.' This is not a good use of people or their time.

For certain types of meetings (and with practice you will know when this is appropriate) structure the discussion by asking each person around the table, in turn, to make the points they want to make. If you know your group, you will know who should speak first, who last. This sort of structured contribution is a good way of eliciting points on which there is wide agreement, where you need to either find or declare consensus, and for challenging individuals to bring as much value as they can to an agenda item. It works particularly well for me after a presentation, but before a set of actions are decided, to elicit weakness, inadequate information, as well as strength of argument.

Ultimately, the most important thing is to summarise. That is the Chairman's job and no one else's. We discussed, we made some decisions, and here is what they are. These are the actions that follow. Effectively, the summary creates a minute of the agenda item that sets the course of action. I always admired the summaries that John Browne produced at the end of each agenda item of a meeting he was chairing, and I try to emulate this.

If you watch me during a meeting that I am chairing, I am always taking short notes, but in my notebook I have reserved a space for points that I will want to use in my summary. As we get closer to the conclusion of an agenda item, I am revising these, combining points, looking over my other notes to be sure that I have not missed something important. This is demanding work, and not to be done casually. It can be done for a ten-minute item or a three hour single subject meeting. Good summarising is rarely done successfully, and yet it adds so much to the feeling of accomplishment people have when they leave the meeting.

When I was 'evaluated' by my fellow directors on my performance after my first year as Chairman of AEA Technology, one of the feedback comments was that they really appreciated the summaries I did at the end of discussions. Indeed, I think that how well the chairman summarises the meeting or agenda item outcomes is what distinguishes an adequate chairman from a real leader. And you know which you want to be.

WEEK 20

Changing Jobs

Someone once asked me why I thought I had been successful in BP, and upon reflection I said that it was because I wasn't ambitious. I loved the first job I had, and thought I could be perfectly happy doing that job for a long time. So when the Vice President to whom I reported suggested a different job to me, I was surprised and pleased, but I didn't think it was something that I had to have or that I deserved as a reward.

In a company, or in the civil service, where people destined for success change jobs regularly, it is possible for individuals to get very confused about what they are doing at work. Am I here to do this job, today's job, really well and achieve something of importance, or am I here waiting to get the next job, which is a step on the ladder to the ultimate job I really want?

This is particularly true because of the historic distinction of line roles and staff roles – or jobs where you were supervising people, running a business, achieving financial goals, versus jobs where you were supporting someone, working in a corporate role, strategising, or planning. I saw many bright people, put into staff positions, bide their time until they could get back to what they thought was a real job. They had been given a job that had a huge opportunity for learning, and they wasted that opportunity.

I think it is a pity that we give bright people very little preparation on how to make the transition from one sort of role to another. And this is especially the case for the line-staff switch. I have done this switch several times. The first was when I was in a university position, as a dean responsible for half a dozen departments, lots of students, etc. Every day was filled with events and meetings and problems to be solved. Then one day I switched to a role that was completely a staff support role for the senior leadership. And the calendar was empty. How do I fill my day? What do I do? The answer emerges, but gradually.

And again, in BP I went one day from having 425 people reporting to me to having half of a secretary. When you have 425 people, no matter how good the organisation and the other managers, every single day there is a staff issue that needs your attention – whether it is finding a next job for someone (!) or a staff member who wants leave to try out for a football team, the death of a child in a traffic accident, or someone found drunk under the diesel tanks (all of which actually happened).

Remove this part of the workload, and suddenly all your time is your own, in a manner of speaking. Actually, all the time is the company's, but you have to decide how to fill it.

I think that this is a very disorienting transition for most people, especially the first few times. By the third time I did this, it was great. I had a lot of things I wanted to think about, and do, and at last I felt I had time to think, to plan, to work on ideas.

So a short plea, that among all the sorts of management courses we offer, one little segment should be devoted to this problem of staff versus line roles, and how to be effective in both. Leaders offering someone this sort of job change should please think a little bit about what sort of coaching is required, and how to set objectives for the new job.

One other observation about changing jobs: it sometimes happens that people are moved far too quickly from one job to another. This is a disservice to the corporation, unless it is an emergency situation, and it is a disservice to the individual. If it happens more than once to the same person it can have long term, negative consequences for their career. They are denied the opportunity to build a track record, and instead they become a person who fills a management role that has suddenly opened. To stop this, an HR leader with a strong voice needs to be able to say 'No, we will solve this another way.'

Jobs are opportunities for learning, both about content and process. The content learning curve is steep in the first months; for most people it slows but never stops. It includes content about the business situation, about its technical underpinnings, about the competition, and the forces that drive the market. But it also includes knowledge of the people in the team, their strengths and weaknesses;

the network of people inside and outside the corporation with whom one needs to interact effectively. What a pity to invest in building this content knowledge and not take the rewards of that investment by keeping a person in the job long enough for them to make an impact.

Process learning comes more slowly, and more steadily. Each of us has to have the opportunity to experience novel and difficult situations at work, do our best to deal with them, and learn from that experience how to do it better the next time. Much of this is transferable from job to job; there is great value to being able to repeat the experience to get the learning deeply internalised. Almost all of us have, at some time or another, tried to learn a physical technique or a sport, and would accept without question that the 'process' needs to be practised over and over again until it can be done with little conscious thought.

So it is with management, and the techniques for doing it effectively. When we take a person from one job to another too quickly, we immediately give them a big content learning requirement, and process learning is pushed to the side. There is little time to practise, correct, and practise again. The result is senior managers who know an inadequately small amount about many things, and whose skills at dealing with people and themselves are also poorly developed.

WEEK 21

Building Best Teams – Part 2

I once went on a BP course called Building Best Teams. A group of about 15 of us, from various parts of the company, worked with two very skilled people, Roy Williams and Dick Balzer, both of whom knew the company (and most of us) very well.

And what was the essence of what we did for three days together in a nice country house hotel? We worked on giving and receiving feedback. Yes, we did a lot of other things, and learned a lot of other things, but the one thing that ran through all the exercises and presentations and learning that we had during that week was how to give and receive feedback.

Some years ago, I studied Japanese. Someone told me that you can only understand the Japanese by understanding their language, and that is very true. Because at the heart of this language is levels of respect, as it is in Japanese culture. Thus there are many verbs for giving and receiving in Japanese. If you give something to a pet you use a very different verb from giving to a child, or for giving to a servant, or to a peer, or to your boss. Likewise with receiving. Only if we can get the subtlety of the language, deep in us, not memorised, can we also be adept at integrating into the culture.

So in our Building Best Teams course we all realised that we needed to learn, or relearn, the language we used in talking to others in our team, in giving feedback to colleagues, and, when asked, to our boss. Right down to our pronouns (when to say I and when we, for example). What should be done in the group, and what should be done in private. When to be gentle, when to be firm. I have been through several mergers and know now that when I work with teams that are integrating is a time when I must be most sensitive on giving feedback, and that I have failed at it several times. How to give feedback is a skill that must be learned and practised, and you need to be very self-critical about your own performance. Indeed, we need to get feedback on how well we do this.

And how to receive. To understand when it is a time to sit and listen and learn from what is being said to you, and when it is a time to discuss and get more clarity, or even defend. How to be pleased to receive criticism rather than be hurt by it. Mostly, the first law of receiving feedback is to keep your ears open and your mouth shut.

How to give and receive feedback is not instinctive, and most of us don't learn how to do it in our families, when in school, or, for that matter, most of the time in the teams of others. It may be that some sports team coaches are very adept at giving their players feedback, but I doubt that there are many who want any feedback themselves. How to give and receive feedback is either the essence, or close to the essence, of team building.

FOR THE WEEKEND

Travel

When I was a child we had a set of phonograph records called 'Little Songs on Big Subjects'. It included lessons on the universality of blood types, the fact that Jews were involved in the American Revolution, and the value of travel to broaden ones experience.

I flew on an aeroplane for the first time when I was 20 years old. My children all flew before the age of two. As a young assistant professor travel was limited to a couple of meetings a year, in such exciting places as Columbus, Ohio and Pittsburgh, sometimes Los Angeles – oh the thrill for a Brooklyn boy of landing there for the first time, walking out of the terminals, and seeing a long road lined with palm trees. I had never seen a palm tree except in pictures. Later, I got better invitations, and even as a faculty member went to some exotic destinations.

In 1973 I went to India for the first time. My research was sponsored by the US Army, and they were none too happy about paying for a trip to India, as the United States had been on the opposing side in the war which led to the creation of Bangladesh as an independent country from Pakistan. Nonetheless, on the promise that I would write up some specific impressions of the state of research in India, they bought me a cheap ticket. The good news was that I was going for a one-week meeting, and the ticket required a stay of three weeks, so two weeks of sightseeing were required. Well, sightseeing and a little science at various academic institutions around the country. The cheapest ticket was on PanAm's around the world flight, PA 002. It left New York, and, making a large number of stops, flew to Los Angeles. So I reached Delhi by way of London, Frankfurt, Beirut, and Tehran.

We American boys, at least of my background and generation, and I guess still many today, grew up so unconscious of the world. I had never been outside the United States, indeed did not have my first passport, until I was 24. (When BP and Amoco merged in 1998, many of the Amoco senior management did not have passports, and almost none had ever lived outside the Midwestern US.) Completing my Ph.D. in June 1966 I went to New York, got married, and a couple of weeks later left for Switzerland to spend a year as a postdoctoral fellow at the Eidgenossische Technische Hochschule (ETH). I spoke a little German, very little, and had no idea what life would be like. Of course, it is Switzerland, a sort of epitome of conservative (at that time very conservative) civilisation, so not a terrible culture shock. But at least I was around people with different ideas, I spent my day (at least after the first few months) speaking

German and listening to German spoken, and I travelled, to Italy, where the toilets were unlike any I had ever seen in my young American life and where, in 1966 farming was still being done with teams of oxen; to Germany, seeing Dachau and being around Germans and German science.

But none of that prepared me for three weeks in 1970s India. For lepers, for beggars who had been intentionally mutilated as babies, thrusting their deformed limbs through the window of your train carriage, for being in the temple in Madurai where 10,000 people eat and sleep, pray and make music, for conversations with Indian pilgrims. To be in India then was to experience an immersion in a country dominated by religion and its consequences, and I moved among the hordes of people up the mountain to the Jain holy site at Shravana Belgola, seeing the feet of the great statue of the Jain hermit Bahubali anointed with coconut milk, and sat lost in thought in the magnificent temple at Halebid.

I had a carefully planned itinerary, fly to Delhi, then immediately on to Bangalore, not yet transformed into the IT city it is today, for a week of science. Then north again to see Delhi, Agra, Kajarahu, and Calcutta, and back to Delhi to return to the US. Unfortunately, when I arrived in Delhi, and had made my way over to the domestic terminal for my flight to Bangalore, I discovered that there was an airline employees' strike in progress. My flight was going, it would be flown by executive pilots of Indian Airlines, but because I had not been there three hours in advance (an impossibility as I was still in the air!) my seat had been given away. Then I experienced the kindness that I would know many times from people in India. A man, seeing my plight, spoke to me and told me what to say to those at the counter so that I could at least be considered for a seat on the flight. He told me that there were plenty of places, and the staff only wanted to be sure that they gave the places to the most important people, so I had to make myself important! I did exactly as he told me, of course. Local knowledge is the only thing that counts in such a situation. Eventually I did get on the plane, surprising the local hosts when I arrived in Bangalore.

But of course all my carefully worked out travel plans were scuppered by the strike. Fortunately, during the week I met Annette Tardieu, a French scientist, and we agreed to travel together, improvising a trip around South India. Of course it is another wonderful lesson – plan, make good arrangements, but when circumstances change abandon them and do something different that might be even better than what you planned.

We had to travel by train, and were warned that it would be best to travel first class. There were only two classes on Indian trains, first and third. In first you had a nice comfortable compartment, with a bed and food brought to you. In third there were benches with large rivets protruding out in case you wanted to lie down and be comfortable. The only problem was that there were a very limited number of seats in first class, and you could only reserve for a train at the station from which you were departing. So from Bangalore to Cochin was no problem, our local hosts took care of that, but after that we would be on our own.

Our Indian hosts advised us to use the following strategy: When we arrived at the station, go to see the station master at once. Tell him that we were Professors, introduce ourselves, compliment him on his station, ask to see it in more detail, while informing him of our need to travel from Cochin to Trivandrum two days later, in first class. This method actually worked, but it was very time-consuming, as we spent nearly two hours drinking tea, conversing with the station master, and touring his fascinating domain. When we got to Madurai some days later, it was very late at night, so we went directly to the hotel. The hotel manager asked us about our plans, and we told him we wanted to go by train, first class, to Madras in two days, but had no reservations. No problem, he said. Of course there are no seats available, but we will get tickets for you tomorrow. There would be a small fee. The fee, when put in terms of our time, was about 50 cents an hour. Thereafter we used that method exclusively.

So it happened that I saw the old Jewish settlement in Cochin, swam in the sea at Trivandrum, went to the Meenakshi temple in Madurai, the beach temples of Mahabalipuram and Kanchipuram in Madras, tried to go to Ramiswaram in a typhoon, but ended up sitting in a railway car with Indian pilgrims talking science and philosophy with their leader, who simultaneously translated to the pilgrims surrounding us as the storm raged. Eating with my hands, wading through water waist deep to get from railway station to the hotel across the street. And spending hours, days, and nights with Annette talking about everything, as we travelled.

•

A year later, in 1974, I went to Bulgaria. The Cold War was still in the deep freeze, Nixon had just resigned as President. This time the Army was quite interested in paying the bills, and in hearing what I had to say about Eastern European science and scientists. I stopped off in Paris on the way and saw Annette for a few days of frolics, ate and drank too much old Calvados, then flew to Sofia. It was my first visit 'behind the Iron Curtain', and I would not return to Eastern Europe or Russia for nearly 20 years, until 1993, after the fall of the Soviet Union. My young Bulgarian hosts met me at the airport, though my official host was Professor Simova, head of the Institute, and a member of the Central Committee. Over dinner they asked 'Is there anything you particularly would like to do or see or buy while you are here?' 'Well,' I said, 'I hear that there are some very nice Bulgarian folk carpets, and I would like to buy one to take home with me. But I suppose they are quite expensive.'

'Oh no, not expensive,' they said. But they looked worried. 'The problem is that right now no carpets are available.' Hmm, OK, no carpets available, too bad. I had no other requests. This phrase, 'unfortunately very few are available', was one I heard often in Bulgaria. When we were travelling during my visit, and would stop for lunch, inevitably we were given big menus. I asked for translations, and then would say, well, perhaps I might have the chicken, something like that. 'Oh,' my hosts would say, 'perhaps it is not available. But in this restaurant you will get a very good sausage from the Macedonian region, we suggest you have that.' After a few such experiences I watched what was happening more carefully. As we came in to the restaurant, the guys looked around. Everyone was having the same thing for lunch. So when the waiter came, you ordered what you saw everyone else having, as the rest of the menu was 'not available'. This was not always the case. If we were with Professor Simova, the restaurant manager would immediately appear, clear away any other people who were waiting for tables, and seat us himself. Then a variety of dishes would appear, none of which were being served to anyone else.

The conference in my field of research was for all the scientists in Eastern Europe, including Russia, sponsored by the Academies of Science of these countries. Each Academy invited one Western guest – I was the guest of the Bulgarian hosts, and the only American, along with one Brit, one Italian, and one Frenchman. The Yugoslavs were present, treated as something in between Eastern Europeans and foreign guests.

American visitors were a novelty in Bulgaria in the 1970s, and I was only 32 years old, so as a young American man, even more of a novelty. We flew to the Black Sea resort of Slanchev Bryag (Sunny Beach) where the conference was to take place. A reception would be held that evening, and I went to my room to change. I dressed for an evening party, the weather was mild and I wore a blue blazer with a silk paisley lining. If I say so myself, I looked good, especially in a country where people did not have access to stylish clothing. As I came down a young woman scientist from the conference was waiting for me. It was a characteristic of Eastern European science at that time that there were many more women scientists than in the

US or Western Europe. Anyway, Sonia was waiting, though it was not clear if she was a scientist or an 'administrative aide'. What was clear was that her job was to see to it that I was not walking around unescorted. Indeed, in the three weeks I was in Bulgaria it was difficult to ever go out alone. As we walked out of the hotel, she touched my blazer and remarked on how beautiful it was. Then, as we strolled over to the reception she said in somewhat halting English, 'There are many women at this conference who will want to sleep with you. Please select someone appropriate.' I did not really want to ask her if I had heard correctly or perhaps she could repeat. We just walked on. In fact it did not happen; perhaps the woman, Marusia, who I did end up spending quite a lot of time with, was not 'appropriate', but we did manage to have some wonderful, intense, conversations about our very different lives, and exchanged little notes and cards for several years.

Later that night we were in a night club, loud music, Russians drinking as if their vodka supply might be cut off at any moment (which it wasn't). And we started to talk about politics, sports, cars. The band was finishing a number, and the person sitting next to me said, 'We will talk again when the music starts.' It was in places like this that the Bulgarians or Russians liked to tell me underground jokes, and hear American jokes as well.

The Russian culture of consumption of alcohol was not limited to night clubs. At the conference, when the morning break occurred at about 10:30 am, I looked for coffee, but found that everyone else was having a morning brandy. One morning a group of us, all the non-Bulgarian delegates at the conference, were taken to the nearby town, where the mayor presented his plans. He was questioned closely by the Russians who were present, and afterwards, seeing that he apparently had given satisfactory answers, vodka was called for and one of the Russians made a toast. Great, I thought, and made as if to leave. Then the mayor made a toast in return, followed by toasts from all the other countries represented. I decided that as I was the only American present, and my fare was paid by the US Government, I would bring greetings from the President of the United States, and toast US–Bulgarian friendship, which was pretty much non-existent. This was very well received. Then, when my legs were barely able to function and my nose was completely numb from the vodka, I was presented with a small medal in honour of my visit. I was told by one of the Russians that it was inscribed with the words Peace, Work, Socialism. I still have it. In the car on the way home we passed a large factory, and to make conversation I asked the Yugoslavian scientist sitting next to me what it was. He replied, 'You know that medal you are wearing, Peace, Work, Socialism? Here is where you find the work.' When we got back I fell into a deep sleep, and the next thing I knew someone was banging on the door, 'Professor Bulkin, Professor Bulkin, you must come, we are going out this afternoon.' It seemed it was time for the tour of the brandy distillery!

My visit had occurred not long after Nixon's resignation, and this was a subject of great interest to all the Eastern Europeans. But the theme of their questions was not about the causes of his resignation, Watergate and so on, but rather 'Where is Nixon now? When do you think he will attempt his return to power?' I tried to disabuse them of this notion, but they were very persistent, not able to imagine that an ex-ruler who was not in prison would grow old peacefully. Finally, in one of these conversations, the delegate from England intervened. 'Look,' he said, 'think of Nixon now as a non-person, like Khrushchev', and that stopped all further inquiries along this line.

As we were travelling back from the Black Sea to Sofia, by train, we stopped in Plovdiv, a very old city with excavations dating back to antiquity. As we were walking through the old town we turned a corner and my face lit up. There was a store with dozens of beautiful carpets hanging everywhere.

'Ah, the carpet store,' I exclaimed.

'Sadly not,' Nikolai said, 'this is where people bring their carpets to be cleaned.'

The day before I was to leave, we were in Sofia, and two of the guys from the lab came by my hotel. 'We wonder if you would like to take a walk?' they inquired. Now after three weeks I knew that taking a walk was because something was to be discussed that they preferred not to be overheard. At the Black Sea we frequently went for little walks when they wanted to ask questions about life in America. Now they had a special request.

'You know the book by Gray?' they began. This referred to a book by my friend and colleague the late George Gray, of Hull University in the UK, a core book for the field in which we were all working. 'Of course.' 'Unfortunately this book is not available in Bulgaria. We order all our books via Moscow, and we have ordered this several times but it never arrives, so unfortunately it is not available.' Well, I did not know what to say about this problem, but they had an idea.

'We would like to propose something to you. When you get back to America, perhaps you could buy a copy of Gray's book. In England there is a man who sells equipment for Unicam, and once a year he makes a trip to Bulgaria. If you will send him the book, he will bring it to us. In exchange, we would like to give you a present of a Bulgarian carpet.'

So it happened that the next day, as I flew out of Sofia airport back to New York, I had a rolled up carpet with me. Probably from the floor of one of their apartments. Professor Simova was at the airport to see me off, and thanked me for my help with the book. 'Such nonsense,' she said, 'that we cannot get it.' So even the establishment did not support the established rules!

I followed instructions, sending off a copy of Gray's book to England, and about four months later received a little handwritten note from Nikolai, thanking me for my Christmas present which had just arrived. I did enjoy informing George Gray when I next saw him that he was banned in Bulgaria.

•

It was not just in the Soviet Union that the workers were adept at defeating the system. When I moved to the UK in 1988 the telephone exchanges had not yet been modernised. They involved large numbers of relays, that, when tripped, had to be found and reset by hand. Partly as a consequence of the antiquated exchanges, there was a shortage of lines, so there was a long wait to get a phone at home.

Getting around the system to be at the head of the queue to get a phone installed was relatively easy. My colleagues gave me a script that I had to use when speaking to the telephone company. It involved my stating that my job involved supervising people working on hazardous materials, that I was the senior executive of this division, and that I had to be available day and night to be called in case of emergency. By following this to the letter my phone line appeared the following week.

About a month later, I came home to find that the phone line was dead. The next day, from the office (now remember this was before mobile phones), I called the phone company, and they told me that I had to go home and meet the repairman there. Sure enough, he arrived a few hours later. He showed me that there were two bare wires running into the house that carried the telephone signal and the power, and that because it had been windy these wires had wrapped around one another. He climbed up the pole, untangled the wires, but of course that did not restore the service. He now had to go to the exchange and find the tripped relay and reset it. Now he explained to me that they were replacing these bare wires with a single insulated cable, but the policy of the telephone company, at that point not yet privatised, was that this replacement was only done when the wires had wrapped around each other three times, and this was number one.

Sure enough, in about six weeks there was another windy day, the same thing happened, and the same guy appeared. As he climbed the pole I mentioned to him that this was number two, and I guessed we would have to go through the same thing again before he could replace the cable. As he got to the top he said, 'Yes, that is so, but there is an exception, and that is if one of the wires has come completely off the pole in the wind' and so saying, he gave the wire a hard pull and it fell to the ground. Smiling, he came down, took out a roll of cable, and installed it.

Systems, processes, procedures, rules . . . whatever you want to call them, there are none so good that those they are intended to control will not undermine them. I have seen this over and over again, and not just in India and Bulgaria. I am sure we all have anecdotes from our business careers about how people at many levels in the organisation subvert the system when they do not find it sensible. Yes, it is the role of management to make the rules, to be sure appropriate procedures are in place and followed, but failure to listen, to think about behaviours, to be sensitive to the needs and desires of the workforce, will ultimately mean that the system loses to the people. This is not about stopping dishonesty or theft – your employees are overwhelmingly honest – rather it is about establishing and modifying processes so that the processes and the leadership are respected.

One of my favourite anecdotes is about a man on a business trip: Half-way through the trip he is walking down the street and his coat is splashed with mud, resulting in it being badly stained. He has it dry cleaned that day, and when he returns he submits the dry cleaning bill as part of his expenses. Back comes a note from his boss, saying that it is company policy not to pay for personal dry cleaning, please redo your expense form accordingly. He writes a polite letter back to the boss, explaining the circumstances, that he had to call on important customers and could not arrive with a dirty coat, etc., and attaches this to his unchanged expense form. Back comes a note, this time from the boss' assistant, attaching a copy of the policy that personal laundry and dry cleaning are not reimbursable. So the man sits down and redoes his expenses, this time attaching a yellow Post-it note that says 'The coat's in there, you find it!'

WEEK 22

Materiality – Too Small to Matter

I was once in a meeting with John Browne, quite a few years ago when he was the Managing Director responsible for technology in the corporation, listening to a review of a series of projects underway in our US research centre. I had heard these projects reviewed before, several times, but it was John's first exposure to them.

The presenter had gone through a fairly long description of a project on a particular corner of electronic ceramics, when John asked just how big might the market be, or how big might we expect this business to ultimately grow in revenue.

'Well, our medium term goal is $25 million, but we expect it ultimately to grow to $100 million.' John was clearly not sure he had heard correctly and asked 'Is that revenue or profit?' No, that would be the sales, but we expect to get a good margin.

I think that is the last we heard of that project, and several others.

In a company with sales of $200 billion, derived from a few products, it is not sensible for management to be spending time reviewing research projects that might (and we know there is always a lot of optimism) grow to $25 million. Nor is it rational for the leaders of the technology programme to run such projects.

But they do, and it is a disease of R and D, especially corporate block-funded R and D, to engage in exploring ideas that lack materiality. I became a non-executive director in a company with $400 million in sales, in two main businesses, and found management and the Board spending time on projects off the main business line where the five-year plan after commercialisation was to grow sales to $5 million. Problems of materiality are very scalable, and this disease can flourish in companies of all sizes.

Of course (as with everything else in business), there is an exception, and it is a major one. There are companies that are big, but that have hundreds of thousands of products. Two examples of this are 3M, and GE. In this case you run projects to develop products that might be $25 million in sales in a multi-billion-dollar corporation, because the corporation has literally hundreds of thousands of such products.

And finally, the trap. Corporations often look at products in a company like 3M, and their R and D process, and think, oh, look how successful that process is in bringing forth innovation; we should copy what they do. But the process is usually a total mismatch because there are few 3M's, and many companies that need to grow a few core businesses so that they are number 1 or number 2 in the market. This is best done by being innovative in and around those core businesses, and by finding ways to do the core business more efficiently and effectively. A completely different kind of R and D programme, in other words, but one that can pay real dividends that are material.

WEEK 23

Offices and Symbolism

We all have an image of the office of the chief executive. Spacious, with plush carpet and dark wooden furniture. Some rich, deep-red curtains. Besides the big desk, on which there is not very much paper, an area with a sofa and a couple of chairs. Or perhaps a small table in a rich oak or mahogany around which several people can sit for a mini meeting. Carefully arranged antiques or original art are usually part of the vision.

Where in the headquarters building is this beautiful office located? Usually around the top floor or just below, in a secure setting, where you have to get past a guard, then a receptionist, then past his or her secretary. It is a place designed to inspire awe in the junior staff member who may occasionally visit this domain. It gives an impression of importance to external visitors. Perhaps it is also designed to say this is a rich and prosperous company, just look around you.

Now there are many problems with this vision in practice. Besides inspiring awe in the organisation, it also sets a standard and an aspiration. If the CEO has 700 square feet and a private bathroom, original expensive art, antiques and plush carpet, then what must his business leaders have? Something about 80% of that? And if he is rather remote and hard to get to, shouldn't they be as well?

I remember taking over management of a Division when I first came to the UK, and the man I was succeeding told me that the secretary was excellent, because she did a great job of keeping the staff away from the office.

As BP underwent cultural change in the early 1990s, it made many innovations in offices. Imagine a transition from a headquarters of 35 stories to one of only eight stories, of which one is the medical centre, and one is the cafeteria. Then have the CEO and his direct reports sit on the 4th floor, rather than up at the top, and allow people, unless they are pretty suspicious looking, to just walk right in.

The offices themselves are pretty modest, light coloured wood – this is significant, think of the image – simple carpeting throughout.

Lots of glass walls for the executives who have offices, and most people working in open plan.

One idea, even for most of the relatively senior executives (say not the top six, but the next 30), is to have very small offices (3 x 3 meters), just a desk, workstation, a few shelves, and then have lots of shared meeting rooms of all sizes, places where 4 to 24 people can sit comfortably. Some with sofas, some with small tables. Simple, modern art in the corridors. All the walls of glass.

There is a great deal to be said for open plan – doing away with cellular offices altogether. The popularity of open plan waxes and wanes, but it has much to recommend it. Sure, it's frustrating to be working on something that requires concentration and have to listen to the person next to you talking to their young daughter about her school trip to the farm. But I think this frustration is mainly worth it for the upside, which is an open interaction with those in the team. A different kind of question, of request for help and advice, comes in open plan. No need to get past a secretary, fix appointments with your own team, rather a lot of informal contact.

And people can and do learn an etiquette appropriate to open plan offices. They learn who can be interrupted and why. Ubiquity of mobile phones allows people to move to a quiet private place for their personal calls.

Open plan can be made much more attractive than it usually is. It works best if there is space, so people are not crowded on top of each other, though for certain teams productivity comes from overhearing others' conversations. Remember Dustin Hoffman and Robert Redford in *All the President's Men*? The newsroom is a model we could all think about in our own office design – maybe it is inappropriate but it is worth considering before rejecting.

Lighting and furniture are important. If it is Corporate Headquarters it should not look like the back office of a third rate insurance company. If it is possible to light areas over desks, and leave corridors a bit dimmer, it creates the feeling of a special space for people.

Above all, offices require thought, and at the highest

levels of the corporation. I often come into corporations and think: this CEO and other Board members got the headquarters that an interior designer told them they wanted, rather than that they told the interior designer what the office tone and character needed to be. Don't miss the opportunity that offices offer to make statements to everyone in the organisation about what is important.

WEEK 24

Good and Bad Behaviour in Mergers

In 1987 BP took over the minority interest in Sohio, a company for which I had been working for less than two years. BP had owned 51% of the company for some time, but let Sohio function with its own processes and objectives. Now, with the acquisition, everything was to be merged into one.

Sure enough, teams descended on us to integrate. Some of them were great, they listened to what we were doing, looked for what was of interest and value to the new company, looked out for good people as well, and generally took us through a gradual transition process. But others were terrible. They started with the presumption that there was the BP way and the wrong way, and we had better get going on moving over to the BP way quickly. Moreover, when we talked about achievements in our projects, they conveyed a clear message that there was already someone in BP who had cracked that problem or was tackling it in a better way. Often, as I soon learned, this was spoken with only the most casual knowledge of what the BP group was working on.

Later, when as a senior person in BP I was part of the merger with Mobil in Europe, and later with Amoco, I thought I could still remember the good and bad experiences I had had during the Sohio acquisition, and try to behave properly. But I didn't. I found it was very hard to be appreciative of the other company, no matter how deserving they were of respect. Moreover, when I gave a message, a useful message, I sometimes gave it in a way that was not sensitive to the feelings of the person to whom I was speaking. They did the same thing, and as a result we underperformed for a while.

We do things in a certain way, and become imbued with our way, take a lot of pride in it. So it is hard to have the maturity to step back and look objectively at my way and your way and learn to use the best, or at least to persuade you around to my point of view rather than impose it. But that is what leaders need to do during a merger or even a takeover transition. I have come to believe that, while we are always in a hurry to move things along in a merger, and so we should be, a few days of training for those leading merger teams would pay big dividends. Not just in *what* we are going to accomplish, but in *how* we are going to accomplish it, so that the people from both companies, and especially the ones who will be crucial to its future success, come out of the process feeling valued.

It is the people at the top, for example the two CEOs in a merger, who set the example by their behaviour in front of others. The other senior executives will take their clues from the examples they see, and this will percolate down through the management. When bad behaviour occurs, the senior people will talk to their people and do a little course correction. Some will learn from these experiences and improve; those that don't become part of the cost synergies to be achieved in any merger.

WEEK 25

Know your Boss

I was preparing a paper for an executive committee once and, having written it, thought that it would be great to start it with a quote from Spenser's *Faerie Queen*: 'Be bold, be bold and everywhere be bold . . . be not too bold.'

So I did. And this was a great hit. The CEO of our business really liked it, and it became a theme for the meeting. Thus encouraged, I occasionally used other little lines from Shakespeare, or the occasional joke to liven things up. This worked well, and people really seemed to appreciate that the presentations I gave were not as dry as others.

But a couple of years later the boss had changed, the whole executive committee had changed, and I was still doing my thing in the same way. Now it all fell flat. No one laughed, no one seemed to appreciate it.

Sure enough, it emerged that the new boss hated it when people included that sort of thing – literary quotes, etc. in presentations. I don't know why, exactly – perhaps because he didn't know any, perhaps because he felt it was not business-like and serious. Someone told me that I was lucky not to have lost my job over it.

So there is a good lesson here, about knowing and understanding the boss, in a deep way. Listen to what he or she tells as a joke, and also hear the silences, such as the lack of jokes.

And anyway, it is a bad idea to keep doing the same routine over and over again, like a tired variety show performer. What worked was not the quote, but the fact that I differentiated myself from other presenters by using it. That was what I really wanted to accomplish, and I should have realised this myself.

SUMMER

'Summer has set in with its usual severity'

Coleridge

SUMMER

WEEK 26

Cross Cultural Communication

Andre was the intellectual leader of BP's operations in southern France. For nine years, while we owned a minority interest in this as a joint venture, we had little ability to find out what they were actually doing. During this period, the group under his leadership developed a revolutionary new process for making polyethylene. They knew, of course, that if BP had been in charge they would not have had that much time to work on something.

(There is a side lesson here, which is that most new technical developments, the big ones, not the incremental ones, require much longer than one supposes. If you don't have the patience to stick it out, better not to start).

So after we took over control of the venture, we learned that there was a new polyethylene process. A team from London came down to hear about it, and the French group were prepared to proudly present their achievements. Here is how it went, according to Andre.

'A group arrived from London, and we all sat down in our large conference room in the research centre. The BP guys all opened their blue notebooks, which we have learned that they always carry with them. Then the leader of the BP delegation addressed me.

"We have some questions" he said. "First, who is the Project Leader?"

"Project Leader? Project Leader?" I said. We all looked at each other. "Perhaps we could have a five-minute break while we discuss this." After five minutes we returned to the room and said, "Well, there is no Project Leader, in fact there is no project. All we did was invent this new way of making polyethylene." You can imagine that they were very upset.

And that is the way our communication has been with BP ever since. They always come down here and ask the wrong questions.'

It is very hard to adjust your style, your tone, your mode of questioning, things which are the essence of how you behave in business, to a new cultural setting. Yet failing to do so will reduce your impact. I have seen secondees from the US come into a meeting in Brussels involving oil company representatives from across Europe and completely misjudge the volume, the bluntness, and way to listen if they are to make their points effectively. And this is the easiest case, same industry, meeting in English, pretty much the same sets of values around the table.

Now if you cannot make that work, how much more difficult to do it in Singapore, China, Russia, Indonesia, Argentina. In a way, it is very difficult, because you have to unlearn behaviours that have become instinctive, but in another way it is not. You just have to stop, take extra breaths before speaking, watch how others are speaking and how they are listening, and listen extra hard yourself so you catch the innuendo as well as the surface meaning.

Then sometimes, if you can adjust to the local tone and way of doing business, you can have your home behaviour – be it brasher or calmer, more or less threatening – as a weapon in your negotiating arsenal, to be taken out and used to shock people into a decision.

WEEK 27

What's your Objective?

There is nothing more basic to management practice than setting objectives – specific, time defined, measurable, achievable yet stretching, relevant to the main goals – and yet somehow we often forget to do it systematically, and this is a big mistake. If someone comes to talk to me about a new job, whether inside the company where I am already employed, or from outside, the first question I want to ask is 'What would you expect me to accomplish in the first year? What do you think my objectives are?'

If I have taken over a new department or organisation, the first thing I want to understand is what everyone's specific objectives are for the coming year. How do they align with my own, which I hope I have already agreed with my boss?

The process of setting objectives makes everyone think about what they are going to accomplish, why they are coming to work every day. It should facilitate dialogue across the department and between the manager and the team. Objectives make you ask the question 'Whose help do I need to get done what I want to get done this year?' and conversely 'What is my role in accomplishing what the team needs to accomplish to be successful?'

I don't think it matters if one is in a big corporation or a small company, or in a charity. Having an annual discussion about objectives, setting them, reviewing progress two or three times a year, and then an annual appraisal, is a good discipline that should not be neglected. When things go well, objectives are accomplished and everyone feels good. You enthusiastically move on to the next level of performance. When things don't go well, you have something against which to measure how badly they went. If an employee is to be rewarded, you can do it against exceeding expectation on set objectives. If a team member is not working out, you have something in writing which provides the basis for what can be a difficult discussion.

And don't forget to do this at the highest levels as well as at the intermediate and junior levels in the company. There is certainly no better way of ensuring alignment than having well-crafted specific objectives from top to bottom in the company. Too often in big companies senior executives think that personal specific objectives are only appropriate to the junior staff, while at the senior level it is all about corporate objectives. I think that is wrong, and is a missed opportunity for performance and development.

Sure, you are flexible, and there is nothing inviolate about a plan for the year. Opportunities arise, plans change. One of the best reasons for having a plan is to know when you have deviated from it. Having specific objectives does not constrain flexibility in any way. You just sit down, assess the situation, decide what to drop and what new objectives to agree, and move on.

WEEK 28

Getting to Know You . . .

Supposing you are given responsibility for a segment of the business, or a functional role, that involves overall managerial responsibility for 100 people. What's the first priority, after your predecessor (assuming he or she existed) has cleared off?

You might be tempted to sit in the office reading the notes that he left you, or reading through what you were told were key files. Or maybe you think you should ask your key subordinates for some numbers to try to understand the state of the business. Or perhaps have a meeting of your direct reports. All good things to do, I suppose, but not, in my view, the number one priority.

Businesses succeed because of people – and they fail because of people too. So if you want to know what is going on, talk to the people. Who are the leaders, both in terms of team leadership and as individual contributors, among the 100? Find out, and make a lot of time in your diary to speak to each of them individually.

So often I have seen managers who are a year into the job, and are yet to have a one to one conversation with many of the key people in their organisation. The 20 hours that you spend doing this in the first two weeks will pay great dividends. You will learn – if you show that you are open to listening – what excites them, what frustrates them, and what worries them. Themes will emerge, and so will red herrings. You are the leader because you have the brains to sort one from the other.

Armed with what you have learned from these conversations, you can begin to think about what you want to change, what are your goals, and most important, who is going to be crucial to achieving those goals. When you start to work on staff development, you will know who is itching to move on to another role in the organisation, and who wants to stay there and do the best possible job in her technical speciality.

There will be some people in most organisations who are too junior in grade to feel comfortable coming to chat in the boss's office. And anyway, you need to get out of the office. A good challenge for anyone taking over an organisation is that by the end of the first two weeks (unless you are dispersed too widely in the world, in which case three weeks) you should have been into all the work places for which you are responsible.

Think about your manner, what you are looking for; find out in advance what is going on in each room and who is working there – at the bench, the terminal. Talk about safety not in a judgmental but in a questioning way. See who is around early in the morning and late in the evening, not to take attendance but to get some idea about workload and motivation.

Not only will you learn a lot by doing this, it is a lot more stimulating and fun, and a lot more memorable to you and to the people you meet, than reading papers in your office.

WEEK 29

Working through Influence

John D Rockefeller modelled the organisation of Standard Oil on the two models of organisation he knew to work: The United States Army and the Catholic Church. These are traditional hierarchical models, and hierarchy became the norm for company organisations for most of the twentieth century. In this model, authority and accountability are everything. Ultimately, the chief executive has authority over all the employees of the company, and is accountable for all aspects of its performance.

The model sets aspiration for the individual. Having authority over a larger number of people is better than over a smaller number. Having a bigger budget is better than having a smaller one.

Dare we challenge this model? After all, it has been widely used and seems to have stood the test of time. Still in many companies in the last 15 years, an alternative has emerged. And that is the model based around influence.

It says that what we really want, for our most senior and gifted employees, is the ability to influence the direction of the company, and its outcomes. This is also what they want for themselves.

But if you are running a big organisation, hundreds or thousands of people, it is very difficult to have influence beyond the part of the company that is your area of accountability. Lots of people mean lots of people problems, and no matter how good the managers in the business, no matter how excellent the Human Resources function, the person in charge has to deal with lots of these people issues. These are important issues, they affect lives and careers, and how well they are handled determines in large part how employees feel about the company. The leader of a business entity or a big technology centre must deal with safety, customers, community relations, environmental performance. Every day becomes filled with these issues. I know from my own experience that with 500 people, doing the essential things in business means that time for thinking about strategic issues is reduced to near zero.

Increasingly, companies have begun to create posts at the most senior level, in corporate headquarters, that have very few people reporting to them, and a huge responsibility for influencing the direction of the company. These may have titles like Chief Economist, Chief Scientist, Vice President for Operations (not running operations but putting in place policies and practices to ensure their excellence). The posts rely on the quality of the individuals in them, on the networks they have built up in the corporation over time (so generally must be filled by those with internal track records) and on access to the CEO and other directors.

They work by influence. Difficult to measure, sometimes, but you know when someone has it, and when it is working, because the right person is much in demand by the organisation, and the wrong one is always trying too hard. The right person in these roles knows what he or she wants to achieve, how he thinks the corporate agenda should be moved forward, and undertakes activities to make this happen. The right person is sought after for ideas when the CEO is thinking through a new corporate direction, or putting together ideas for a speech to articulate that direction.

Mergers can strain the system. Companies that may be a perfect business fit often have very different cultures regarding individual influence and authority. When BP and Amoco merged, one of the senior jobs went to a fellow who was in the same role in Amoco, and there he had 600 people working for him. So he thought, in the larger company I will surely need to have about 1500 people, and he was very happy with this. But several of us sat with him and said, we have a different model, decentralise, let the business run most of these people, and you have a small central staff so you can keep control of the big issues, and still think about where this part of the company is going.

Oh the crying that ensued. It was as if we were attacking his very reason for living. So back and forth we went, until in frustration he asked to see the CEO, John Browne to tell him how we were ruining his ability to function. John listened to him and then asked him a simple question:

'Do you want to have influence in this company?' Well, now he was appealing to a different side of the personality, although the poor guy did not yet know this. Why? Because he had in his mind a simple logic, the more people who work for me, the more important I am, and hence more powerful, therefore more influential.

But when he said, of course he wanted to have influence, that is really what he wanted, John said to him, 'Then give away all your people. Because then you will have time to think, to bring ideas to me, to go around the world and show people different ways of doing things. '

A 21st-century corporation makes space for people who work through influence rather than through authority and hierarchy. In doing this it also makes space for innovation. What's more, individuals earn their influence, so it shows that the company is a rigorous meritocracy. Now some people will never be comfortable with working this way; they can still be valuable to the company, but it sets them on a particular career path. More dangerous, and also evident in mergers, is that some senior executives have trouble dealing with individuals who don't represent a big organisation in the company. It is hard to root out this problem, but it is worth having antennas that are sufficiently sensitive to pick this up.

Oh, and the person whose story I told you, the one who wanted 1500 people working for him? He wound up with about a hundred, was totally preoccupied with matters involving them, and was gone from the company a year later.

You do not need the CEO to do this for you; serious people can do this for themselves if the spirit of the company is sympathetic. Going into a new corporate job ask yourself: What do I need to make this happen? Do people need to be working for me or could they be embedded in a business unit? Is much of the organisation I inherited crucial to achieving my goals, or (even if they are doing valuable work) would I be better off giving these people away so I can focus on what is important?

Few people take initiative to make their own organisation radically smaller. Done with a strong rationale it can allow you to be much more productive and influential.

FOR THE WEEKEND

Leadership Learned on the Back of a Horse

On a late summer afternoon, about five months before my retirement from BP, I sat on the patio of a friend's house looking out over the Montana plains, sipping a beer and chatting. Several riders came into view, their horses walking along slowly. Then they started to trot, and soon they were cantering away into the distance. I had never had a riding lesson in my life, but it seemed such a beautiful thing to do. I asked our hosts if they rode, and they said no, too dangerous. Still, when I was back in London and reflected on it I realised that it had been more than a decade since I had any new physical accomplishment, not since I had learned to do archery with some proficiency.

In March 2004 I had my first riding lesson at a nearby stables, and when I had learned the basics I moved to another, larger riding school. I worked with teachers, Catherine, Paolo, Vebeke, Maria, Sarah, Sid, and many others. It was Paolo who had the most influence on me, and from whom I really learned to ride well. But you can learn things from all teachers. And on those mornings, whether in the school or riding through the woods of North London (yes, there are woods in North London!), I came to understand that riding, probably any physical activity that you learn and master, holds many lessons for our lives. Here are some that I remember.

Equitation – 1 Motivation

The first challenge is to make the horse move forward.

Catherine, my first teacher, says: Give a little kick that says start walking forward. The horse looks around but does not move. Now what? Kick harder? Well, that is one idea.

Paolo says: think, what if you kick harder and it still doesn't move, do you kick harder still? Surely there is a better way.

Paolo says: don't kick, that's what ignorant teachers tell you to do. Just squeeze with your legs. If he doesn't move, squeeze again. Repeat the signal. After three times tap with the whip. Not a bash, just a tap. Don't get frustrated. Eventually he has to move, but if you get frustrated because he is not doing what you ask you will not get a good result. Tap again with the whip. And again. And again. See, he starts to walk.

Paolo says: You want the horse to move forward, but he is thinking that he has other things he wants to do, like eat some more breakfast.

How do you motivate your team members to move forward? What is the counterpart of a squeeze or a tap? And how do you get the combination of focus and persistence that gets everyone aligned and moving towards the goal? A leader needs to try some approaches, and if they don't work, try something else, while trying to keep the frustration under control.

Equitation – 2 Commitment

Catherine asks: Are you going to keep riding in those shoes, or are you going to buy a decent pair of riding boots?

If you are going to learn to ride, you have to make a commitment. A commitment to being fit enough to ride, with enough strength in your legs and enough flexibility in your arms and back to use them effectively to steer the horse. And a commitment to have the right equipment. You can't just turn up each week, borrow a helmet, ride in any old outdoor shoes and jeans. At the very least if you are going to ride you have to commit to buying your own helmet, a decent pair of boots, and a school whip. Do some stretching every morning, and some bicycling to get the legs a little stronger. Oh yes, it is every week that you are going to have a lesson, not once a month.

If you are going to learn to ride, you have to make a commitment to it. In any job, any role you take, you must make a commitment and evidence that commitment.

Equitation – 3 If I'm Not in Control, it Must be Out of Control

Paolo says: Let the horse go out of control. Don't pull back on the reins when it starts to move faster, just let it go.

But this is a little scary. The faster it goes, the scarier it is.

Paolo says: You have to learn to let the horse go, that nothing bad will happen if you are not in control every single second. And if you give it the signal to move forward faster, but then pull back on the reins, you are confusing the horse. What do you want me to do, go or stop?

You give someone a job to do, and you have to let them do it. If you have a demanding leadership role you cannot possibly be in control of everything that is going on, and sooner or later you will realise that that is a good thing.

Equitation – 4 Looking Ahead

Paolo says: Why are you looking down at the horse? When you drive a car do you look at the bonnet (hood)? If you look down at the horse you will not see where you are going. Better to keep your eyes on the horizon, or at least look where you are going so you avoid collisions.

So many of us are looking down and not at the horizon. You can't lead if you are looking at the desk.

Equitation – 5 Conscious Incompetence and Conscious Competence

Three of us are riding out one Friday morning as usual, a lovely day for a ride in the woods.

Barry is due for a single lesson, but there is a problem, the person due to teach him has not shown up, and Maria is short of teachers.

Maria says: Barry, why don't you ride out with everyone else, it's such a beautiful day.

Barry says: Oh, I don't know. I'm not too good with the canter.

We all urge him on. Don't worry, you can always trot, and besides once you are in the woods the cantering is much easier.

It takes a few minutes but Barry is won over.

As usual we walk the horses into the woods, then trot up the first hill.

Sarah says: OK, ready for a short canter?

Off we go, down the long straight trail. And here comes Barry's horse, having left him behind on the ground. Oh dear, he meant it about not being ready to canter.

Another time Paolo says: You have to think about your legs, your arms, your eyes. Don't press with your feet, be light, and keep them pointed straight. Keep your elbows at your side and your hands up. Look ahead, not down at the horse. OK, now move forward.

Paolo says: OK, now you are moving, you still have to think about your feet, your arms, your eyes. Every time I say 'your feet', think about what you are going to do for two seconds, then make the adjustment. Same with your arms, your eyes. Don't adjust the instant I say it, have a two second pause while you think about it, then do it consciously.

This is rather difficult. There is a model of behaviour, especially applied to the diverse roles that an executive has to fulfil, which says you start with unconscious incompetence (don't know what you don't know), move on to conscious incompetence, then try to break through to conscious competence, where you are performing well but need to think about it, you take those two second pauses, and finally to unconscious competence. I don't think there are any shortcuts, but you do need to know where you are in the journey, and how quickly you need to get to the next stage if you are going to achieve what is required of you.

Equitation – 6 Taking a Scary Step

Paolo says: Don't mount up by holding the back of the saddle with one hand, and the front with the other. Instead, put your right hand on the front of the saddle, and gently rest your left hand on the mane, now look ahead, as the horse is doing, put a foot in the stirrup and mount up. This is gentler on the horse's back.

But Paolo, thinking about doing it that way is a bit scary, it feels like I will fall.

Paolo says: Good, do it anyway.

Paolo says: OK, let's learn how to tack up. Hold the

reins and the bit in this way, with your three fingers holding these three leather straps. Now keep your hand flat on the bit, like so. Good. Now you put your thumb into the horse's mouth here, because at the back of the mouth there are no teeth, and when you put in your thumb, the horse will open his mouth. Then you slip in the bit by pulling upward.

Do I have the courage to put my thumb in his mouth? Probably. But of course once I do it, I rush to shove in the bit and jerk up my other hand.

Paolo says: Patience. Do it slowly and smoothly. Why are you rushing? If he turns his head away just bring it back. You are going to do this.

In a leadership role you may be required to do something difficult, and it is all right to feel that this is scary. Growth comes because you overcome those fears and do it anyway, with competence.

Equitation – 7 On Safety

Vebeke says: What are you doing? I answer, I am tightening my girth, and adjusting my stirrups.

Vebeke says: You have one foot in the stirrup, and one out, and that is not safe. Always you must have both feet in or out of the stirrups.

That is sensible. Of course that is how to be safe. So why didn't anyone ever tell me this basic safety rule before?

Safety is a big part of your job. And it is important to show, or have someone show, everyone how to do the job correctly. That is what safety training is – how to do the job properly. We must take the time to do this.

Equitation – 8 On Preparation, on Self-Reliance

Before setting off to ride, in the woods or in the school, adjust the stirrup and tighten the girth. The girth is put on when the horse is in the stable, and they have a great ability to puff out their stomachs, so that what seemed tight is now loose.

The beginner has an assistant from the school, or the teacher, adjust the girth and the stirrups. Move your leg so I can check the girth. How are the stirrups, are they even, too short, too long?

Paolo says: You have to learn how to do your own girth and stirrups. Just put your thumb under the buckle of the girth, take the strap in your hand, and pull up. Use your thumb to hold onto the buckle, and see, it slips right into the hole. Now the stirrups. Pull up on the strap, use your finger in the same way, and push down with your leg until the length is right. Now slip it into the hole. Hold the strap out away from the horse, and press down as you pull it up, until the buckle is at the very top. Good. Now the other one.

What a great pleasure it is to be competent to do the basics myself.

Sometimes there are simple things that we need to do on a regular basis but, for whatever reason, don't learn how to do. I have seen executives who cannot put paper in the photocopier, or deal with some common email problem.

Technology evolves, and what was once someone else's job is now a basic task. You wouldn't ask your partner to tie your shoelaces, or would you?

Equitation – 9 Planning a Turn

Paolo says: If you want to turn, turn your body in the direction you want to turn. No, not at the last minute, but well in advance. Then the horse will get the message and will follow, turning in the same direction. And you can reinforce by just moving the rein outwards, with a little squeeze. No, not pulling back on the rein.

Paolo says: Make a business plan. I am going to ride from A to B, then turn right to C, then left to D, and back to A. OK, when will I turn my body? Not when I am already at B; that is too late.

Ok, people use business language because they think we relate to it. And riding a horse in a figure 8 around the school is not a business plan. But, like looking ahead instead of looking down, it is a series of events that you know will occur, and you must plan your actions so that they happen successfully. Much like every day in the office.

Equitation – 10 Change is the Only Thing you can Count On

Maria says: I have you on Flossie today. I ask, what about Flash, that is who I have been riding, we are used to each other. Maria says: You need to try a horse that is more challenging.

Weeks later, when I am used to Flossie, Maria says: I have you on Harley today. I ask, what about Flossie? Maria says: Harley is more challenging.

Maria says: You are on Dolly, and Martine is teaching you today. But, I have been doing my lessons with Sid. Maria says: Sid is gone, try Martine, she is very good.

Every lesson is a tripartite relationship, student, teacher, horse. But for each, the perspective is that he is the only thing that is constant, and everything else is changing.

You get used to things, a particular organisational structure, or a boss, or even an office environment. But keeping it the same, year in and year out, does not usually lead to better performance. A leader will push individuals, teams, even the whole company, to change and change again. And to learn that change is the only thing you can count on.

Equitation – 11 Problem Solving

I am having trouble keeping Flossie from wandering off the track.

Paolo says: Who is the teacher?

You are of course.

No, who is the teacher?

I don't know.

Paolo says: You know who the teacher is, it is the horse. He is giving you problems to solve, and you need to solve them. Make a plan. Think about what you know. Then solve the problem. Are you just going to get frustrated? Are you going to blame the teacher because he has given you a problem that is too hard to solve? No, just try patiently to solve the problem.

Equitation – 12 Always Learning

Sometimes I think: One day my lessons will be finished and I will just be able to ride well. I ask Paolo how long it takes to be able to learn to ride well.

Paolo says: Well, you will need two or three years of lessons, but then you will be good.

But I see that almost everyone continues to take lessons. With the others, I ride out in the woods, trot, canter, and enjoy myself. But then we all return to lessons. Because there is always more to learn. There are subtleties and techniques. There are ways of keeping skills you have learned in shape, rooting out bad habits.

My colleague Gary Grieve and I were once returning from a three-day senior management course, both of us a bit reflective on our experience. After a time he said, 'Well, once a year we go to the doctor and get a complete physical check-up. So it is probably a good idea that once a year we get a check-up on the way we do our jobs as well.' Bad habits creep in, they are like minor infections that are treatable but can get out of control. As well, there are new things to learn, new techniques that can help you be more effective. It is a short-sighted corporation that stops investing in the education of senior executives.

Equitation – 13 Habit Forming

We are taking Flossie back to her stall.

Paolo says: Be careful, just when you get to the stall she will suddenly go very fast.

Why does she do that, other horses don't have that habit?

Paolo says: Because her stall is in this corner, and whenever she is going in this other horse, Pepsi, leans out and bites her ass. So she learns to run fast.

An employee learns quickly that if he says A then you will answer B, so he will not say A or he will run very fast if he does not want to hear that answer. We all need to become conscious of our own habits, and the habits we instil in others.

Equitation – 14 Scary Things

My horse Toby is a joy to ride in the woods, but there are a few things that frighten him. Like a plastic bag blowing around. I say to Catherine, who is taking me out: Isn't it strange, hundreds of pounds of very strong horse, and he is frightened by a little plastic bag.

Catherine says: Yes, sort of like me and spiders.

We all have fears, horses don't pretend about theirs.

Once when I am riding Toby three dogs come running out of the woods right at the horse. He rears up in the air, and somehow I manage to stay on. The instructor quickly has me bring him back so that all the horses are close together, and they find safety in the pack. Gradually I feel him calm down, as we walk on ahead.

About half an hour later we are back at the stables and I dismount. Toby turns his head to nuzzle into my chest, something he has never done. After a fright, even a horse needs a cuddle.

Can you take the time, please, to remember this about your team members? There are things that will happen that they will find very frightening, sometimes rationally sometimes irrationally. It could be a presentation, or a meeting that has had a big build-up, or a trip to a country known for its difficult environment. Your job as leader is to sense these fears, and deal with them in a caring way.

WEEK 30

The Fundamentals

Every business has fundamentals underlying it. Businesses operate in a market, which is why they are businesses, and unless the management of the business has a deep understanding of the fundamentals it is not managing the business, it is simply performing a custodial function.

When I came into BP I learned that virtually the entire senior management of the company had, at some point in their careers, held a leadership role in the supply and trading business. Some people from outside that business thought of this as a mini-mafia, bringing along their friends. I had no idea really.

Then, when I was responsible for 'manufacturing, supply and distribution' and began to see all of this business from the inside, I realised why these people had moved to the top of the company. It was in supply and trading that you learned, in a deep way, what really moved the markets in which our company operated. It was from here that the company had to deal with OPEC and its members, with our large and small private competitors, and with Governments. The supply and trading people learned, sometimes from hard experiences, what were short term fluctuations and what were long term trends. In other words, while doing the business of buying and selling oil and oil products, if they were good and smart, they learned how the markets really worked.

John Browne was the first leader of BP in a long time to come from a different route, through exploration and production. He also was BP's Treasurer at a rather young age, and from that position had insights as to how currency trading was a fundamental part of our business. But he brought another aspect of understanding of fundamentals to the company that had been lacking in the previous generation, namely, that if you are an oil company you had better be excellent at finding oil.

Beyond the importance of exploration, while the supply/ trading people understood the global forces very well, they did not understand or appreciate the market around massive capital expenditure nearly so well. When a company spends huge sums on new capital investment (and in the case of a large oil company this is more than $1bn *a month*) the entire industry of large engineering design and construction contractors is crucial to success. Companies like BP, heavy capital companies, are judged by their return on capital employed. To paraphrase Peter Drucker, those coming up through the trading route had deep insights that helped to build the right things, and to that John added deep insights about how to build the things right.

If a business is to operate at the cutting edge of strategic insight in its markets, the leadership needs to have this sort of deep understanding. Does this imply that a Chief Executive must come from within the company, or even the same industry? Certainly not. But it does mean that the Board, in selecting a Chief Executive, needs to know just what sort of knowledge and insight that person must have. Personality, management and leadership skills, track record – all these are important, but without an understanding of the context and vectors for distinction in which a business operates the chance of failure is great.

WEEK 31

Policies – Less is More

Just as individuals accumulate files, companies accumulate policies. In earlier times, if you entered the office of an executive, one bookshelf (it might be the only bookshelf!) in his office would contain eight or ten big binders filled with company policies. So, in principle, if he wanted to know the policy on bribery he had only to look on page 222 of volume 7 or some such place. Today the same sort of voluminous policies exist in a less visible place, namely on a set of intranet web pages. This has the added benefit of allowing offices to be smaller.

But what if we took a more radical approach? Suppose all the business policies of a company (as distinct from detailed HR policies) were contained in a relatively small booklet, with large type. Could it be done? Of course, it is just a matter of considering what is important, then setting down what you believe in a few clear sentences that everyone can understand and remember.

It is always a good idea to move in this direction; it is essential after a merger or a series of mergers because instead of one company's policies you now have several. Everyone will come with a different idea of what is acceptable, what is important, and what, if you do it (or don't do it), gets you fired. A healthy debate allows the executive to agree corporate values and the policies that flow from them. I assert that the whole set of policies can be set out in a 32 page booklet, but once you subtract photographs and title pages the actual writing is only on 21 pages! And that includes the opening statement from the CEO.

Policies embody the essence of what a company stands for. Here is an example: to be competitively successful and a force for good. Sounds hard to argue with? Well, it actually takes quite a lot of thinking and debate to come to such a statement, and it certainly takes a lot to live up to it. BP and several other companies have shown just how hard it is in the last few years!

Five policies in a booklet of 20–30 pages will suffice – ethical conduct; employees; relationships; health, safety and environmental performance; and control/finance. For each policy there is a corporate commitment and a set of policy expectations. Everyone in the company, throughout the World, is expected to live by these. No exceptions.

I discuss some of these in more detail in other essays, but here just emphasise the great power that comes from a 'less is more' approach to policies. People will pick up and read a small booklet, cover to cover. They will remember statements like 'we will never offer, solicit, or accept a bribe in any form' or 'our goal is simply stated – no accidents, no harm to people and no damage to the environment'. And as managers they will be able to communicate these clear, concise policies to their staff.

The policy commitments and expectations are absolutes, but life does not occur with such absolute clarity. So they also become a basis for debate and discussion. When there is an expectation that says 'Everyone who works for us can expect to be fairly treated', what does this imply for a team recreational or social activity that may exclude some members? How does the policy on bribery fit with our practices on extending and receiving corporate entertainment? Debating questions such as these is also healthy and characterises a vibrant, open, and transparent corporation. When corporate policies fill volumes, as they still do in many companies, no one sees the possibility of debate. When they are concise and direct, they allow space for intensive discussion.

As with many things, we start with an ideal of 20 pages of policies in total, then find that for some of them we need to say more. So be it. But if instead you start with 20 volumes of policies and add to them as necessary you will inevitably have something with much lower impact.

WEEK 32

Managing With and Without Grades

Nearly every big company feels that employees must have a grade, that their position must be defined by a number and a title. So in investment banking a new bachelor's degree enters as an analyst, gets promoted (or not) to associate, then vice president, managing director, etc. We have grading systems for scientific and engineering personnel, for managers, for secretaries. Of course, tied to grade is (presumably) accountability and (almost certainly) reward.

Behind these grading systems lie a whole lot of processes, varying by company but always substantial. To start with, you cannot have grades for employees unless you have standards that define and differentiate each grade. Otherwise grade progression just becomes a reward for 'time served'. Revisiting these standards, not once in the history of the corporation, nor every year, but from time to time, helps to refresh our understanding of what skills and competencies we consider to be important.

There are large consultancies, such as Hay Associates, that are very happy to work with corporations on their grading standards. They will promote large exercises in which each grade is evaluated according to various criteria, and points (Hay points) are assigned. The best thing that can be said about such exercises is that they are not a complete waste of time. The point scoring will satisfy some, though not most senior managers. What is worthwhile about such an exercise is that as a consequence of having the debate and discussion, a senior management team can come to a consensus about what it really considers to be important, and about what differentiates one job or employee competence from another.

It can also learn that in some cases there really is no clear basis for differentiation. For example, I have seen five secretarial grades combined into two, and nine senior management grades combined to three.

There is also process required for determining who is promoted. In some companies it is as simple as a manager going to see her boss and recommending an employee for promotion, a brief chat, a form to HR, and the job is done. I don't think this is particularly useful as process, though it is efficient. If it is worth having grades, and I am not sure it is, then it must be worth investing more time in deciding on movement between them. For this, a management committee must sit regularly, with proper documentation, and discuss promotions.

Through this process, around real employees in the company, everyone learns the criteria and the standards for a grade. This learning in turn leads to much better feedback from managers to employees about their prospects for promotion, or what they need to demonstrate to achieve the next higher grade. It is also a particularly important process for new members of a management team, whether coming through internal promotion or external recruitment, or through acquisitions.

I also favour publicizing promotions within the workplace. In BP in the US this was standard, but in the UK no such publicity was done, the feeling being that the promotion was a private matter between the employee and the company. The great value in putting a notice up or sending out an email to announce a promotion, is that it conveys to the entire group the standard that is expected. By the way, it is also a challenge back to the management team making the promotion – will it pass the 'notice board test', that is, will everyone, seeing the announcement, say 'of course, makes sense to me, she did a great job and deserves this' or not. So what we want is not just a notice saying 'Joe Bloggs is promoted to Senior Team Leader' but something like:

'I am pleased to announce the promotion of Joe Bloggs to Senior Team Leader. [*what has he been doing?*] Joe has been leading the automotive lubes marketing team for the past three years, during which time [*what did he accomplish?*] this team has launched four new products, more than double the rate we have achieved in the past, and [*why is this important?*] consistent with our objective to move ahead of competitors on product introduction rate. [*but we expect more than this at his level*] Joe has also been active in promoting BP through more than 20 talks at local high schools. He led the task force on improving our procurement processes. [*And for his next act*] In his new role, Joe will have responsibility for the expanded industrial and automotive lubricants marketing program that is now in place. Please join me in congratulating Joe on this well deserved promotion.'

Now that is a notice that sends messages.

Of course, we can differentiate between employees without having grades. Companies both large (e.g. Bell Labs) and small have managed without grading professional employees. It is still possible to highlight achievements, to differentiate in terms of financial reward and other symbols of status, and of course it is possible to deal with poor performance. Just because we have the heritage of John D Rockefeller (see Week 29. Working through Influence) in many corporations does not mean the company needs to have as many grades as the Army. I wish more companies would examine the large number of grades that they have to see whether these are really in service of a performance goal for the corporation. Grading is a manifestation of hierarchy, and as I have made clear in Week 29 and in Week 7. Flatten, Flatten, Flatten, I am not convinced that it gives the best result.

WEEK 33

The Discomfort Index

When the temperature goes up, and the humidity does too, we get pretty uncomfortable. To measure this, meteorologists developed the Temperature–Humidity Index, also known as the Discomfort Index. Now, as we know, discomfort can have very different effects – it depends on the person, the context, and of course the level.

Then again, what is very uncomfortable in Minneapolis or London might be just normal weather in Miami or Houston. So there is something about what makes you uncomfortable which is based around your upbringing and (air) conditioning. I had a roommate in graduate school, John Lyford, who, on a really hot day, when most people just didn't want to move, would go out and play 18 holes of golf.

Some people become more productive when they are uncomfortable. In other cases, what appears to be productivity is really just rushing through a job to get it done quickly and remove the discomfort that the boss is causing. For most people, there is often a certain level of discomfort which increases productivity, but if you go beyond it productivity falls off abruptly. The skilful leader takes risks with discomfort, but keeps the door open so he can take the temperature back down again.

If 10 of us are sitting around in a room discussing a problem, and if they are my own team, I need to know who will become a better contributor to the meeting if I make him uncomfortable about his contributions, or his behaviour, or his attitude, and whose contributions will diminish if I do this. As a leader I need to be sensitive to who will respond well to being made uncomfortable in front of his peers, and who will only respond to a quiet word outside the meeting. This is a key part of the competency to build best teams.

Dick Balzer, a long-time BP consultant, and probably the most skilful person I have ever seen at reading the room, uses this to perfection. In a session of any size, he seems to know just who to push in front of others, and who should be going for a walk around the grounds with him during a break. And he knows that for the same person, sometimes the former approach, sometimes the latter, is appropriate.

But discomfort comes in many forms. I was doing a warm-up icebreaker session for a group of about 15 BP senior managers once, and suggested that they put all their papers and notebooks on the floor, and close their eyes. About half thought this was great, and responded at once. Of the remaining ones, some put down their books but kept their eyes open, and a couple were quite willing to close their eyes but not let go of their notebooks. Did it make any sense to insist? No, of course not (though I needed some prompting from Dick Balzer, who was in the room, to realise that). The session would not be more useful for anyone if they were uncomfortable because I had taken away their security blanket. As simple as that: when appropriate, it is more useful to make a suggestion than to give an order.

All this seems pretty simple, but like a lot of simple things, it is hard to achieve. When we have a team that we work with week in and week out, we usually get to know what the most effective tool is. But managing a meeting, sometimes with people being encountered for the first time, sometimes with people from the company you encounter only occasionally, is much more difficult. Yet if you are going to get the most out of the 'team', figuring out what the optimum discomfort index is for each individual's performance, and for the room as a whole, is a great skill to learn and practise.

FOR THE WEEKEND

Housing

What is there about buying and selling houses that brings out the worst in people? Buyers, sellers, lawyers, banks, all of them have the ability to turn from being perfectly rational, decent people into animals when it comes to real estate transactions. Still, house buying and selling can be looked on as a chance to sharpen your negotiating skills and learn a lot about how people will behave under the duress of a deal situation. These transactions also make you learn that even what appears to be a relatively straightforward, routine event, can have surprises that must be dealt with. Complexity is not always in the detail of the deal, it is in the people with whom you are doing the deal.

My first house, 39 Prospect Place, Brooklyn, 1971 – Calling People Stupid

Elly and I had been living in Stuyvesant Town, in a two bed-room rented apartment, but with a small baby, and a desire for space, we looked for a house. At that time, the fashion was to move to Brooklyn and buy a brownstone, maybe in need of a bit of fixing up. Often the houses were set up with a rental apartment, so that the mortgage payment could be covered by the rent. As usual, we looked at a lot of houses, and eventually found one about the right size on Prospect Place, on the edge of the Park Slope section. It was being sold by a real estate agent named John Bijur, who, it emerged, was also the owner of the house – sort of.

What Bijur had done was to buy the house from the Puerto Rican family who were living there, signed a con-tract and given them a deposit, but he didn't close on the sale. This suited the family, who needed to find another place to live in any case. What we didn't know, was that what would occur would be a double closing. We would buy the house from Bijur at an appropriately outrageous profit for him, and he would simultaneously use our money to pay off the current owners.

There were complications from the beginning. My law-yer, Bernd Allen, was the preeminent brownstone lawyer in Brooklyn at the time. He had a visceral dislike for Bijur based on any number of closings they had both been involved in. But it was more than dislike. Bijur considered himself clever, and Bernd Allen did not believe that any-one in the Brooklyn real estate market was cleverer than he was. So we had the ingredients required for a recipe of conflict.

The mortgage was arranged through the Maspeth Savings Bank, and the closing was to be at a branch of the Bank. There was some sort of problem regarding my income and qualifying for the mortgage, which almost derailed the whole thing. But somehow Bernd resolved this with the bank. Then there was the question of points. At that time, lenders would provide a mortgage of a certain size at a certain interest rate, but charge points, which meant you actually paid higher interest (or got a smaller loan, same thing) than was stated. It was understood by the bank that the buyer paid these points, but Bernd had negotiated a side letter with the sellers so that they paid half. It didn't seem to be of consequence, but the bank was unaware of this. Sure enough, at the closing, as the bank officer was going through the papers, a copy of this side letter fell out, and the officer picked it up and read it. The lawyers and the bank officer then adjourned to a back room, while we sat with our baby, and the Puerto Rican family, waiting for them to sort it out, which they did. Not everything that is said in a deal needs to be said in front of everyone.

There were innumerable small items to be paid for. I had been instructed to bring a cheque book with lots of cheques, the New York tradition being that the closing was held face to face, and each of these payments, except for the big cash payment for the house that the bank provided, were made by individual cheques. At some point going through these they came to the site survey, something like $215. I was about to start writing when Bernd looked up and said, 'Survey, what survey, we didn't order any survey.' Bijur was puzzled. 'Bernd, come on, we always have a survey, of course your client has to pay for it, you know that perfectly well.' 'Sorry, you ordered a survey, you can pay for the survey.' Back and forth they went, until Bernd started to gather up his papers and say I guess the deal is off. Elly and I were a little bit aghast at this drama, but of course Bijur folded at once, and said, 'OK, we'll pay the survey costs.' At this Bernd turned to me and said aloud, 'Congratulations, we just gypped these guys out of $215.'

Now I didn't know anything about business back then, or about negotiating, but I did realise that the packing up the papers technique was effective (indeed I have used it myself on occasion to great effect), and that the 'Congratulations we just gypped these guys' line was silly and arrogant.

Country House, Birchwood Lakes, the Poconos, 1980 – Fully Furnished

Susan and I had been thinking about a weekend house to get away from the city with our small children, and the Poconos, a not very upmarket area about two hours from Manhattan, was where many of our friends were buying houses. We spent a few weekends looking around, and eventually found a place on a lake in a community called Birchwood Lakes. The house wasn't great – through some architectural feat it had been built so you couldn't see the lake from any room of the house, though there was a good view of the road – but after consulting with a couple of builders we realised there was a way to make it really nice.

The real estate agent told us the sad story of the house, because it formed part of the deal. It was owned by a couple who had built it thirty years earlier when their children were small. They loved the house, and many great family memories were connected with it. However tragedy had struck. One son had committed suicide, and a second had died of cancer. Now the husband had also been diagnosed with advanced cancer, and had had one leg amputated in an attempt to save him. They realised that they could no longer cope with the house, nor could they enjoy it when it held so many memories of their sons. So one summer week-end they left, thinking they would come back, but once they were home they decided that they could not bear to go back any more, and asked the real estate agent to sell the house. The deal was, buy the house as it was, with all the contents (this included rotting food in the refrigerator). The owners only asked that the real estate agent go into the house and gather up all their personal photos from the walls as well as their photo albums, and pile these on the kitchen table. They would then come by on the way to the closing, pick up these items, spending only minutes in the house, as they bade it farewell.

We agreed. After all, the furniture and dishes were useful as a start, the refrigerator could be replaced, and otherwise the house was fine for our needs. So came the day, we drove to the house ourselves, on the way to the closing which was to take place at their lawyer's office in Milford,

Pennsylvania. Sure enough, the sellers were there. But they were not just picking up the pictures, they were taking all the towels, silverware, anything else they could load into the car. The wife was busy shifting stuff out when we arrived, and her husband, who was not very mobile, was packing it into the car. Of course, when he saw us he called to her, 'I told you not to do it, I knew they would find out' etc. So here they were selling a $40,000 house for cash and with all their troubles she was trying to take a few dollars' worth of old towels. I just looked at the husband and said, 'Now put it all back', and we drove off to our lawyer's office, across the street from where the closing was to take place.

By the time they arrived, we had explained the situation and our lawyer told us to stay put and he would go across the street to discuss with his opposite number. When he came back he told us that the sellers were so upset, so emotional, that it would be best if we did not meet face to face. So all the papers and money were shuttled back and forth across the street and the deal was done. Not long after, we sold most of the dishes and such to a local second hand junk dealer.

The essence of a business deal, even buying a small house, is that there is a rational process of negotiation, appraisal, and legalities. But when someone is emotionally attached to an asset, or to a deal, rationality goes out the window.

17220 Aldersyde, Shaker Heights, Ohio

When I moved to Cleveland to work for Standard Oil, my wife and children were spending the summer in Israel, so I did the house hunting on my own. I had a Polaroid camera, would take pictures and air mail them off to Susan. Her biggest caution was that I not buy a house that was too big, and she kept reining me in. Eventually we bought a very nice house at 3355 Dorchester in Shaker Heights. Five bedrooms, a very nice dining room that seated 12 for dinner, on a beautiful tree-lined street.

The inevitable happened. After six months Susan started to view the house as too small. So even though we hadn't been in it for long, we put it up for sale and started looking for another, larger, house in the same neighbourhood. We found a beauty just a few blocks away, with eight bedrooms, seven bathrooms, a dining room that could seat 20, oodles of space. And a big beautiful garden, with a large patio that had a big awning for parties in sunshine or rain.

The sale and closing went smoothly. The owner was a former professional basketball player with the Cleveland Cavaliers who had overextended himself financially, and owned another house as well as this one, so he sold to reduce his expenses. We were all happy.

But when we moved in there was no sign of the awning. An enquiry was passed back through the real estate agents, who told us it had been taken down and removed for cleaning and storage, no problem, just call this number and get it back. But it turned out that it had been in storage for three years, and the cleaning and storage bills, about

$1000, had not been paid, so it could not be released. Back again to the sellers, sure, they would take care of it, but weeks passed and they didn't. Eventually the real estate agents said we would have to pay the bill, or take them to court.

Well, that is what small claims court is for, I thought, and filed a claim. No lawyers required. On my day in court, they did not show up, and the judge issued a summary judgment in my favour. Now came the problem of how to collect.

The seller pleaded poverty. He told the court that he was unemployed, had no work and no money. There was only one problem with this story: He was doing the play-by-play broadcasting of the basketball games on television, so his employment was very public. I was telling this story to a colleague at work, and he said, look, there is another thing you can do. Take your judgment to the City Hall, and tell them you want to send the bailiffs out to inventory his property to collect your $1000. There is a $5 fee for this.

Sure enough, that got his attention. When a cheque arrived a week later, I cashed it as fast as I could. And retrieved my awning.

The lesson? Well, in doing a deal, a good lawyer will see to it that you settle every detail in advance, even something like an item in storage, because once the deal is done it is hard to go back. And if you are going to tell a lie, like that you are unemployed, don't make it such an obvious lie!

34 Hodford Road, London – Chinese Take Away

We knew that the owners of the house were moving to Florida – what we had not appreciated until after we moved in, and started to receive threatening letters to them, was that they had to get out of the country. They had made it clear that we had to close the deal on a particular day and the cash would be wired to them, so that they could close on their new house in Miami. All fine.

We went to see them two weeks before the closing just to go through a few details. Where the various manuals for the appliances would be left, were there drawings for renovations that had been done, etc.? We had bought a few things from them, among them the safe that they had installed. So I said, 'While we are here, give us the combination to the safe and show us how it works.' The husband went to comply with this request, but his wife said, 'Don't tell him, we still have our watches in that safe.' What? We are doing this deal for $900,000 and you are worried that we are going to sneak in here and steal your watch?

They moved to Florida a few days before the final closing of the sale. I called the estate agent who sold us the property and asked if he would walk us through the house, just to be sure it was left in good condition, things we had purchased from them were left there, and nothing had broken in their move. This is pretty standard in the US, but not in the UK. But we were friendly with the agent, so he said sure, and we went over to the house two days before the sale completed. The house was a total mess. Not just the detritus of movers, boxes and tape and such, but they had obviously ordered in Chinese food and left cartons of it half eaten. Why would someone do this? An extra half hour of effort by a few people would have been all that was required to clean it up. Maybe we sometimes get exhausted by a task and can't complete the last half hour of work that leaves it tidy. Maybe there is a temptation to cheat your customer just a little.

The solution was simple. Get an estimate to have professional cleaners come in and clean the place thoroughly. And notify their lawyers that the cost of that, some $900, would come off the purchase price. Negotiations opened and proceeded until the very last minute, but in the end they agreed. Usually someone will back down. And as a bonus, we learned the value of a professional crew cleaning up an empty house.

WEEK 34

Environmental Issues – Being First, Being Proud

Some issues are specific to a particular company, a geographic region, or an industry sector. But there are issues that transcend all of these, and these are issues around the environment. Clean air, clean water, land free of toxic chemicals, acceptable levels of noise – these are issues of priority everywhere, as they must be for every company. So I ask, 'what does it mean to a corporation to have these as priority issues?'

For a long time companies were not bound by any environmental legislation, and behaved as if they were not accountable for environmental protection. Then legislation began to be put in place, and corporate attitudes changed. Companies took a position that government – through legislation and regulation – decided how much pollution is acceptable, and the role of a corporation was to comply. Their position on the environment was, and in some corporations still is: we always comply with the law, wherever we operate.

But this position is flawed in several ways, and by the mid 1990s companies, especially those operating globally, began to see this and act accordingly. How is it flawed?

First, it allows different standards for operations in different parts of the world, depending on the local legislation. None of us would accept this in safety – after all if we require hard hats and safety glasses in New York to carry out an operation in a chemical plant, we require the same protection in Belgium, Indonesia, or China. So how can we allow discharge of water from the same sort of plant in different countries to carry different levels of toxic materials? I have written elsewhere (Week 14) about cultural and moral relativism. Surely behaviour such as discharging toxic chemicals in one place but not in another is an issue of moral relativism; to my way of thinking it is unacceptable.

Second, it says that environmental issues are about compliance, and does not recognise that in fact they are strategic issues. What do I mean by that? Strategic because taking a leadership position can differentiate one company from another in an industry where the public finds it difficult to tell them apart (see Week 5. Decommoditising Your Business). Strategic too because it affects how the company is regulated and treated by governments, what sort of protests it attracts, how its employees, customers, and shareholders feel about the company.

So there is an alternative to 'we always comply with the law'. And that is 'we need to continuously reduce our emissions'. BP embodied this as part of a simple statement on health safety and environmental goals: no accidents, no harm to people, no damage to the environment, from anything we do. You can't say it much simpler than that. And by saying that we need to continuously reduce our emissions, and acting on that, you translate the goal into company policy. Yes, it is a statement that is aspirational, and one that is doomed to fail – as BP did in several spectacular ways. But aspiration is the only way to achieve extraordinary results.

Now you might challenge my assertion that this is strategic, by countering that it is the easiest thing to copy – if BP announces (as it did) that it will reduce its greenhouse gas emissions by 10%, Shell can do the same thing a few weeks later (as it did). So how can something that is so easily copied be strategic? Because you can't copy being first! The company that is on this path will always see the environmental vulnerabilities, and will, if it is confident, make statements about what it is going to do about them. It will allow civil society to judge whether it is fulfilling its commitments. Others will only be able to follow, and they will *have* to follow whether they like it or not. The first company makes front page news; the others don't make news at all. This is leadership.

There is an important footnote to environmental leadership, and it is about employee pride. Our employees are citizens. They are concerned about the natural environment just like other citizens are. And they want to be proud of the company for which they work. A progressive stand on environmental issues is motivating for employees. Like you and me, they do not want to be on the defensive about their company and the environment. Instead, when we take a stand on an issue such as climate change, our employees can and do talk to their friends and neighbours about what they are doing – in their refinery, or chemical plant, or supermarket – to deal with problems of climate change, local air quality, or clean fuels.

After BP announced its merger with Amoco, John Browne made a point of doing a number of town hall meetings at BP sites around the world to communicate directly with employees about the merger and its implications. At the first one, a refinery, the first question posed to him was this: BP has a very different position on climate change from Amoco. Can you reassure us that the merger is not going to affect this? John commented to me the following week that he thought that was interesting. It became more interesting when the same sort of question came up at every other town hall meeting he did. It was then that the impact on employee pride of our stance on climate change really hit home.

As the merger progressed, we did a lot of surveying of employee attitudes, with employees of both BP and Amoco heritage. When we asked employees to rank the issues that they felt were most important for the new company, BP heritage employees put 'Stance on Environmental Issues' as number one, whereas for Amoco heritage employees it was well down the list.

In my experience we struggle so much to build employee pride and loyalty in a big company, to make our employees feel proud to be part of the larger enterprise, beyond their own site or operation. Progressive leadership on issues of importance, like climate change, can have a huge impact. But you have to believe it, you have to act on it not just talk about it, always being sure that your words are more than backed up by actions.

And as many companies have learned, the hard way, environmental leadership is not easy to achieve, and even less easy to sustain. The NGOs that push our companies to higher standards of environmental performance are not satisfied with the steps we take. They always want more, sometimes more than we can give them. It can be very frustrating for the leadership of a company, feeling that it has made a big step, voluntarily, to get no thanks for that from Greenpeace but only a demand to do a lot more. Be prepared for this, and stay cool about it.

But there is another danger, and that is a consequence of the many, many things that a company does as part of its activities. So a big company may act affirmatively and progressively on climate change, but much of the benefit to corporate reputation and employee pride is lost because of a pipeline leak, an accident at a refinery or a catastrophic failure in deep sea drilling. Again there is a good response to this. The corporation takes a leadership position, and it needs to recognise that this leadership position in one area makes it more vulnerable to attack for its performance in another. The executive and the board need to understand that right up front, strengthening the rationale for always increasing standards everywhere. We take a lead on climate change, and this creates equity for our company and its brand. Let's all appreciate that a fatality in our operations, environmental damage, ethical issues, anything like this, can destroy corporate and brand equity. The higher we raise the bar for ourselves in one area, the higher it is elsewhere, and the easier to trip on the bar. Far from discouraging the bold stand, this recognition helps us to make the whole corporation stronger and more competitive. That BP lost sight of this in its business drive is not, to me, a failure of the strategic role it gave to the environment, but a failure to execute that strategy.

WEEK 35

Give and Take

Many big companies have formal networks meeting regularly to share best practice. Everyone (well, almost everyone) wants these to be more than talk shops, or occasions for going someplace nice to spend a few days with your colleagues from the rest of the world. I have discussed elsewhere the idea of evolving networks into peer groups with accountability (Week 16. Peer Groups), but accountable peer groups only make sense at the more senior level. In big companies networks often comprise technical leaders from around the world, or marketers.

There is a curious phenomenon about networks that I have seen very often. When a group of technical or business leaders get together for a network meeting, trying to learn from each other, I would naively think that everyone has a big motivation to take ideas from the others. After all, if I am running retail shops in Australia and I can hear of an idea that worked well in the US Midwest, I might be able to improve my performance, and reward, by getting back to Australia and implementing it ASAP.

At the same time, there doesn't seem that much motivation to give. I have done something interesting, it is making money for my business unit, but what is my incentive to help you do the same thing in your business unit?

This naïve view of networks doesn't actually happen in practice. Indeed, just the opposite happens. Everyone seems to want to give, and no one seems all that interested in take. I have done something that is very cost effective, or I have found a much better maintenance management system, or I have found a way to increase sales of coffee and doughnuts by 35%, and I can't wait for the next network meeting to get up and tell all my peers about it. But guess what? They are sitting there impatiently waiting their turn to tell the group about the wonderful thing they have done.

If you grew up in the US public school system years ago (maybe they still do this) a part of the primary school class time was something called 'Show and Tell'. My father went to China and brought back this exotic doll that sings happy birthday in Chinese. Whatever. Funnily enough, I can remember several things that I presented for Show and Tell, but I can't recall a single thing that anyone else ever showed.

And that is the way it is with networks. Something has to be done to break out of this syndrome. To me, the way to do this is to introduce a lot more structure into the year. In effect, a network has to have a performance contract with the company. It can be pretty simple. We are the retail convenience store network, and this year our overall goal is to use best practice to get our coffee and doughnut sales around the world up by 30%. We are the maintenance managers, and our goal for this year is to improve reliability by 1 percentage point across our operations, while keeping costs flat. This is the accountability already discussed for peer groups, with a strong focus not just on capital but on operational excellence.

Then the network meeting can be structured around looking at ideas to fulfil the performance contract. And acting on those ideas. This is the way to break through the give and take syndrome, to derive real value from the networks, but it takes leadership and accountability to make it happen.

WEEK 36

Syndicates, Breakout Groups, and Other Overused Meeting Techniques

'OK,' says the session leader or facilitator, 'We are now going to break into syndicates where you will have 45 minutes to work on these questions, please appoint someone to report back to the group when we reassemble . . .' How often we have all heard these words in meetings, and if you look around and observe you will see a mix of torpor, resignation, and for the more imaginative, an opportunity to escape to the outdoors for a while and hope they will not be missed.

Forming break-out groups, or syndicates as they are known in the UK, is one of the most overused techniques in meetings. Yes, they have a purpose, which is usually to get more people involved in speaking, taking advantage of the smaller group size. But I would contend that a really good meeting leader/facilitator should be able to bring lots of people into the conversation without breaking into syndicates. So if break-outs are just a way of the leader saying

'I will fail to involve everyone properly' you should probably find a better leader.

Even more deadly is the report back session. Possibly you had a good discussion in your syndicate; you enjoyed it and found it a worthwhile use of 45 minutes. Now you have five minutes to convey this to the group as a whole. Why? Who knows? This is just the way these things are done. Generally a complete waste of time. I do remember one occasion where my group, having had a great discussion, decided to sing the report back as a rap song. That we did may be the only thing anyone remembered 24 hours later from the whole report back session.

But . . . There is a time when breaking out is useful. I learned this from Roy Williams, one of the greatest meeting facilitators I have ever known. We were working on restructuring a four party joint venture, a meeting of about 15 people, and my bias was that we do all the work together in one room. There came a point where Roy suggested we break up into three smaller groups, and he silenced me as I started to protest. Sure enough, he saw that if we were going to get through the vast amount of work that was required in the time, parallel work was the way to do it. Three groups, each tackling one part of the problem, bringing back their work to the group as a whole, almost as if they were subcommittees.

And Roy was astute enough to know that we couldn't have worked that way from the beginning, because the group as a whole had to establish communication and a level of trust. But when that time comes, if you really want to motor forward on the issues, breakouts can work.

There is a general lesson here. In structuring a two- or three-day meeting, something all executives do, perhaps working with a facilitator, it is your job to question and challenge the techniques being used. Be sure they are really appropriate for the work that is being done, and for the people doing it. And mix things up. Sometimes just a chance to talk to the two or three people near you for a few minutes works – a sort of reflection. Sometimes breaking into groups of three for a walk around outside. Sometimes gathering a small group around sheets of paper on the wall and getting them to draw the answer. Whatever . . . but keep it interesting, and trust your judgement when you think a session is going to become boring or unproductive.

WEEK 37

Shine a Light

Remember the old line about two friends walking down the street, and one of them says, 'Look, there's a $20 bill lying on the road.' The other replies 'No, that can't be a $20 bill, if it was someone would have already picked it up.'

Opportunities in companies are sometimes like that. There can be money available to pick up, but until someone shines a light on the opportunity it just sits there unrecognised.

BP had this experience with its initiative in reducing greenhouse gas emissions, as well as in cost saving challenges. When the company announced its target to reduce its own emissions by 10%, people inside and outside the company started to speculate on how much it would cost. After the reductions had been accomplished a few years later, an audit showed that the effort had generated $650 million in positive net present value.

How can this be? How could there be that much value

available that was only uncovered after the initiative to cut greenhouse gases, in effect to use energy more effectively, and reduce emissions of gases such as methane and Halons? Simply put, almost everyone was busy with other things, and not looking for these savings. And perhaps more to the point, people had accepted a certain way of doing things that was not optimal, but was the way they had been done for a very long time. When you reset the context for the operation, which is what the greenhouse gas target setting did, smart operators find a more attractive solution.

One of my favourite stories in this respect relates to valves on a natural gas pipeline in the western US. In 1999 a group of bright young leaders was doing workshops around the world for business managers about the company's climate change targets. Inevitably, there was one guy who sat in the last row, arms folded, with an 'I don't want to be here' air. Usually the comments were 'This doesn't apply to my business anyway' or 'You guys come here from London and you really don't have the foggiest idea what we do.' When one of my staff returned from doing a workshop in Houston he reported that there had been a particularly troublesome individual in this mould at that workshop.

Sure enough, a week later this fellow, who came to be known as 'Valve Man', called me. He ran a long gas pipeline, and he said he thought he had come up with something to save some greenhouse gas emissions. The pipeline had lots of valves, opening and closing to receive gas from feeder lines, and to send gas out to customers. These valve were pneumatic, they operated on the pressure in the pipeline. And every time the valve turned, it emitted a small puff of methane, a greenhouse gas 22 times more potent than carbon dioxide.

'I've been thinking anyway of replacing the pneumatic valves with electronic valves, and if I did that there would be no more emitting of the little puffs of gas. So I did the calculation the way you showed in the workshop, and I think we would save about 620,000 tons of carbon dioxide equivalents.' I almost fell off my chair. The total goal for the company for that year was 750,000 tons. 'How much will it cost?' He gave me the number, which a bit of quick arithmetic indicated it would cost about $2 per ton.

'Well of course we will do this no matter what,' I said, 'but is there any payback from the changeover to electronic valves? Maybe lower maintenance cost?' 'No, I don't think it's maintenance – let me think about it.'

The next day he called back. 'I figured out the payback. Very simple. Instead of venting the methane gas, we can sell it. This project has an IRR of 42%.'

Here was one of the best opportunities the company had, and it was only when we reframed the problem as emissions reduction that the manager could see how big the opportunity was. That is how you generate a huge net present value from what people might initially have thought of as a cost.

Great leaders are always thinking about how to do this, in areas from costs of compliance, to tax, to accommodation, to procurement. But the job of the leader is to shift the way people are seeing their operations, stimulating the people in the field to find the $20 bills that are lying there.

FOR THE WEEKEND

About the Author, age 1–10

Mrs Klein sits at her desk, in a PS 182 classroom in the East New York section of Brooklyn. For each child in her kindergarten class she has prepared a record card. She is to make the first entry on these cards, on two lines she will summarize her impression of that child, enter a rating of their ability to read and write, and pass the card on to their first grade teacher. It is a hot end of June day; she is only up to the Bs and already is perspiring and feeling her energy sag a bit. She sips her coffee, takes up her pen, and enters S (satisfactory) for writing, E (Excellent) for reading. Then she writes 'Quiet, slow moving boy'. Blots the ink and moves on. Thus commenced the school record of Bernard Joseph Bulkin.

   I was probably a bold, rough and tumble sort of child until the age of 3. I just can't remember any of that. I lived on the farm, where my parents raised chickens for their eggs, and the few pictures of me that were taken during wartime, when there was a rationing of film, show a chubby boy, riding around in the back of my father's truck, holding chickens, collecting eggs, playing with the farm dogs.

Then my parents moved to New York City, and I was jerked out of the country existence into what was known as a 'cold water flat' in East New York, a rough Brooklyn neighbourhood. It was the end of World War II, and at the age of four I started school at PS 182. Whatever confidence I had as a farm toddler was gone. The next pictures of me show a skinny kid, and I remember myself from those early years in Brooklyn as timid, easily made to cry, something of a victim on the streets. And we were poor. Well, at least we lived as if we were poor. The rent on the apartment was $26 a month, and my father had taken a job as a civil servant at the Live Poultry Terminal in Long Island City.

Our apartment was at 723 Blake Avenue, above a barber shop and next door to a Chinese laundry. We secured a smelly kerosene heater to replace the coal stove early on, and not long after that, a refrigerator to replace the icebox, though my parents and aunts and uncles still often called a refrigerator an icebox. Before the refrigerator came, my father and I would go and get a block of ice, or maybe go and see a man who would come to the apartment delivering the ice.

As if things were not bad enough for me on the streets of Brooklyn, when I was in first grade, I realised that the letters in the book I was reading had become doubled and blurry. I told my parents, and I was taken off to the optometrist. I was fitted with glasses, certainly the cheapest, most unattractive clear plastic frames. So now, in Brooklyn parlance, I was a 'four eyes'.

One summer's day, in July 1950, Louis said to me that he knew how we could get some toys. Of course I had no money, having spent my last two pennies the day before, at Louis' urging, to get Nancy to lift up her dress so we could all have a good look at her panties. I told him I had no money, but he said that we would just go to Woolworth's and take the toys. He had done it before and never got caught. This seemed an excellent idea to all four of his little boy gang, so we set out on the five block walk to the nearest Woolworth store. Once inside we separated, and I went around the toy department taking a few small items and putting them in my pocket. So naïve was I that I didn't even consider that someone might be watching us. We had probably been there for no more than five minutes when Louis told us we had better go.

Outside, I was no more than five steps from the store when I was scooped up by a large man, who took the toys from my pockets while dangling me under his arm. Then he scooped up our friend Lenny under the other arm. At that point Louis started to run, and the man dropped us both and took off after him. I saw Louis get caught, and this time the man did not let go. He got Louis to reveal his name and address, and then took him home to tell his parents. I crept home silently, saying nothing, sorry not to have been able to keep any of the toys, though I am not sure how I would have explained their presence to my parents.

It was a few weeks later that Louis' father, overhearing a conversation in his apartment, learned that I had not said anything to my parents of the Woolworth's expedition, and lowlife that he was, he appeared at our apartment the next evening to tell them. I hid myself under my parents' bed and waited for the consequences, which were not long in coming. Of course I was spanked by my father, and given a strong lecture on how wrong this was.

I know from later conversations with my mother that it was this event that triggered her to insist that we had to move from East New York to a better neighbourhood. Of course all negotiations she held on this with my father were carried out in secret from the children, although an increase in the amount of my parents conversing in Yiddish always meant there were things going on that the children were not to know about. It took until some time in early spring of 1951 before we were told that we were to move to Queens, and in early July, not long after I completed 4th grade, we moved to 71–61 162nd Street, a three-bedroom attached house in what was known as the Flushing-Hillcrest section of the borough, sometimes also known as Jamaica Estates North, but that was only for selling houses. Jamaica Estates proper was a community of larger houses, detached, with spacious gardens. I would see the inside of these houses only seven years later. I was nine years old, and for the first time a child of the suburbs. Louis and a lot of Polish boys of East New York were left behind, and all of my friends were now Jewish.

AUTUMN

'O wild west wind,
thou breath of autumn's being'

Shelley

WEEK 38

Cutting Costs is a Never Ending Process

We once did a model of the BP refining and marketing business, not very sophisticated, but good enough so that one could do some interesting 'what ifs' about the business and its competitors. As we played around with this model a significant truth emerged for me: unless we could eat inflation each year through cost cutting, we would lose competitive position. And this emerges as a universal truth across a very diverse set of businesses. All great leaders know it and practise it.

I have seen companies go through cost cutting exercises, take out redundant jobs, deal with excessive property costs, in a big blitz, and then sit back and say, 'OK, now we have done our cost cutting, we can get on with running the business.' This is such a bad approach. True, there are times when there are opportunities for massive cost cutting, for example after a merger or acquisition, or when circumstances dictate moving the business to a different cost base, perhaps when there is a sharp change in the price of a commodity, or a sharp increase in energy costs, requiring management to take measures to compensate. But in general taking out costs is something for all seasons.

Great leaders take out costs when times are good. They keep policies in place that rein in any expenditure that does not add value. Many years ago, I remember reading about how six or eight executives from RCA (a once great company taken over by GE in 1986) would get off a plane together and each head for his own rental car to take him to the same office where all the others were headed. Later that day, the process was reversed back to the airport. Waste in corporations is often just this silly and just this easy to stop.

I have been on flights to Brussels for oil industry meetings where there were three of us present, from different companies, and two, having travelled in economy for the 45 minute flight, would head for the taxi line to share a low cost cab to the place where the meeting was being held, while the third, having flown business class at five times the cost, had a driver arranged to meet him at four times the cost of the taxi. It may seem silly to ask employees of multi-billion-dollar companies to save a few hundred dollars on a short business trip, but it pays off. Not just in the little expenditures, but in the attitude to big ones.

Now there are good and bad costs. Extra rental cars are bad costs. Spending money on maintaining equipment to a high standard of safety and environmental protection is a good cost. But if only it were so black and white! What about a new computer system to help manage the maintenance of a factory? Good cost or bad cost? After all, the factory has been running safely for years with the existing system. We need to get the business leadership into a mode of asking about the value added from the additional expenditure.

That will go some way, but not all the way. Because how business units behave individually and collectively determines how effectively costs are managed. If each of the twelve factories decides it needs to up the game on a maintenance management system, and they all go out and evaluate the competitive systems individually, and come to three different decisions, then each one can feel it has done the best job for its business unit. But for the corporation it is a disaster. Standardisation offers great opportunities for cost savings, and is usually (but not always) done best by a central functional group; but that group needs to be really good, and needs to earn its keep through adding value to the company and its business units year in and year out.

I once visited Tony Anderson, one of BP's greatest refinery managers, when he was managing the Bulwer Island refinery in Australia. He knew that the only way one could make a small refinery such as his be highly profitable was to keep costs under very tight control while making everything run to the highest standards of safety. I was told that if a new manager, often someone seconded from another business unit, came in and asked for an additional staff member in his department Tony would reply, 'Martin, there are only two things of which you can be certain in this life: you will die, and there will be no additional staff at Bulwer Island Refinery.' The evening of my visit, when one of the managers picked me up for dinner with Tony and the leadership team of the refinery, he said, 'This hotel has a really great restaurant. Of course that is not where we are eating, because it is much too expensive.' We had a perfectly nice meal at a place where you pointed to your steak; someone popped it on the grill and slammed it onto the table a few minutes later. I got the picture.

WEEK 39

Getting Advice – The Advisory Council

External advisory groups (these are to be strictly distinguished from governance boards) are popular in some companies today. And they have a lot to recommend them. But in my experience there is a lot to think about before you start. In BP I spent a time working on and with something we initially called the Technology Advisory Board (bad name, only The Board should be using the name Board) and later called the Technology Advisory Council. Later I served on and chaired several advisory groups for companies, universities, government agencies and a venture capital fund.

Where to start? Before you put something like this into place the fundamental question to answer is 'Do we want advice?' This is not a question with an obvious answer. Companies certainly take advice from consultants, both individual and firms (Week 14. Help: Getting Advice from the Dreaded Consultants). But from a committee? And with consultancies we usually are asking for advice about a specific problem, while with a standing committee or advisory council it is ongoing advice. So I ask again, 'do you really want any advice?' Because if you don't, and you have told people that is why you have asked them to help you, they are going to get frustrated pretty quickly.

Of course, there are other reasons for having an advisory council. The usual one is reputation. Getting a group of distinguished individuals (Nobel Prize winners are excellent for this purpose) together and publishing their names on your website and in the annual report is thought to be an excellent technique for reflected glory and credibility enhancement. This is a favourite technique in the world of venture capital backed companies, especially in biotechnology.

This is not all fluff and PR. It can have a substantive role in corporate reputation. Getting the members of an advisory council committed to the company can make them excellent ambassadors. A good group of advisory council members can help deal with reputational issues around stopping of major research projects, closing a laboratory, or relocating work from one country to another. They tell friends and colleagues exciting things they have heard about. They help on promoting the positives and minimising the impact of the negatives.

Connections and relationships are another reason for having an advisory council. The right group of individuals can open doors in other companies, in new geographies where the company is seeking to expand, and in universities. While this might seem to be an individual activity

– one member introducing the company to another – there is something about laying out challenges to a group that leads to better generation of networked ideas.

But suppose you really do want ongoing advice from your advisory council. What is the next thing to think about? You have to decide to whom the council is advisory. For example, if it is a technology advisory council, does it advise the chief technology officer, or his/her boss, or the CEO and managing directors? It is very useful in bringing members on to the council to make it clear to whom they are accountable.

Understanding who the ultimate recipient of advice is does not preclude others also receiving some. For example, while the CEO may be the person to whom the advisory council reports, this may only happen once or twice a year. In the interim, quite a lot of useful feedback might be given to the functional leader – CTO, CIO, etc. who interacts with the advisory council more regularly.

If the format for meetings is one of presentations by staff, followed by discussion, then feedback to those who present is an important component of deriving value from the existence of the advisory council. This should be structured, and it should be clear to those who present that they will get the feedback.

Before we go any further, we need to populate the council. A first question is the balance between external and internal members. For the Technology Advisory Council of BP we started with a structure that was about an equal number of internal and external members as regular attendees. The leaders of technology in all parts of the company attended, and we had six external members. Later, we changed this so that only two internal staff were members, and we had 10 external members. By contrast, I was on an advisory panel for a company where there were only three external members and eight internal.

Any combination is possible, and there is no right answer. But the dynamic of the meeting will be very much determined by this choice. What sort of discussion, who gets how much air time, what sort of actions and follow up occurs, all of these will be pretty much decided when you settle this question. On balance, I prefer a small internal group, strictly limited by logic behind the choice, and a larger external group. But that is a personal preference.

How does one pick the external members? I think there is one key rule, and that is that they need to be a peer group. You cannot have Nobel Prize winners sitting with second tier industrial representatives. But you can have leading people from academia and industry on the same panel, as long as they see each other as peers. Again, there is not a single answer as to who it is appropriate to have, but if, for example, the advisory council is going to meet regularly with the CEO of the company, then it would be a good test to think about that meeting and imagine each potential member in that setting. Amazing how easy it is for potential candidates to fail that test.

A key quality that I look for in advisory council members is breadth of interests. I am happy to have a member on an oil company council from the pharmaceutical industry, as long as he or she is really interested in learning new things, and is insightful about applying knowledge from one industry to another. Academics particularly need to be screened for the breadth of their interests, unless the company is so focused on one business area that they will only hear about a narrow range of topics. I like academics who have chaired a really successful department, or have been dean of a group of departments, and can speak about what is going on across those areas. People with a lot of curiosity are what you are seeking.

Once you know who you want as members, is there anything else to think about? Yes. A few things.

First, who is going to chair this group? What seems to work is bridging the internal and external, and for a public company that bridge is provided by a non-executive director. We did this in BP, and I chaired an advisory council for a company where I was a non-exec. This person should have the right sort of insights and judgement about what is important to the company – strategically and financially; be able to represent the outputs of the advisory council to the Board, and be able to discuss issues with both the functional leadership and the CEO.

Second, how long should members serve? One of the most common mistakes is to appoint advisory council members without specifying a term. I have observed that if you choose the right people they have a lot to give, but after a while you are hearing the same advice that you heard several years earlier, sometimes in a different context, but basically the same advice. So a challenge is to continue injecting fresh ideas and perspectives into the advisory group. To me a three-year term, with an unstated (but occasionally exercised) option to renew for one or two additional years, is the best bet.

Third, frequency of meetings. Four a year is ideal. It does not create an overwhelming burden on the internal leadership in terms of organisation and content, yet gives the advisory group regular contact with each other so as to build their ability to work together productively. It allows coverage of a range of company activities. One of these meetings can include a debrief of the CEO and executive directors.

Fourth, attendance. You choose busy, active people for members, but unless they commit to coming to the meetings it is hard for them to add value. If you have four meetings a year, you expect everyone to try to attend them all, but to at least make three of the four, and not to miss two in a row. It is good practice to tell members when they are appointed that if they miss too many meetings you may ask them to leave the council.

Finally, pay. Yes, members should be paid, and the amount should be commensurate with the size of the company, the time commitment expected, and the level of distinction of the people chosen.

WEEK 40

My Own Voice

During a course on something else entirely, Dick Balzer got us together and said that we had to try some idea techniques, so that we could use them and be comfortable with using them. Senior managers often have little recent training in things like brainstorming, mind mapping, above and below the line charting, etc. and, when they try to do these techniques fumble around with some half-remembered ideas from a session they attended years earlier.

So it is important to add some of these things to your tool kit, learned and practised well enough so that you can bring them out when appropriate. Not a lot, but a few key ones that are always useful. For this some training is needed, some investment of time.

The key point is not what you learn during the course; as with any technique, it is how you put it into your 'own voice'. Each of us, in senior roles in large or small companies, charities, community or voluntary organisations, has a style and an approach that we like to use, that suits our vocal abilities, our nature as a person. Probably quite a lot of this comes from our upbringing, either copying parents or teachers or deliberately doing things differently. Over time it becomes our style, 'our voice'.

Many years ago when I was teaching chemistry to first year university students, I went to a presentation by Hubert Alyea of Princeton, known as one of the great masters of chemical demonstrations, live chemistry done in front of a class. Alyea had things changing colour, exploding, meters swinging and bells ringing, and during some of this hour he sang and danced as well. Of course I came away thinking, well, I guess I can't do demonstrations, because I don't have the showmanship that it takes. But not long thereafter, Art Campbell of Harvey Mudd College came to visit us in New York, and we talked about demonstrations. He told me that he was not a great fan of Alyea, for just the reason of my reaction – he made people think that unless they could sing and dance they couldn't do demonstrations in front of the class. Wrong – certainly you can do them; just do them the way that is effective for you!

When you want to run a brainstorming session with your team, or some other form of breakthrough, it is essential to take what you have learned in a course and put it into your own voice. This is true for the full range of techniques, and applies to all forms of speaking as well.

Like a lot of what characterises great corporate leaders, the key thing is to listen and observe, to learn techniques, and then to think about how to do this for yourself. This is not like rote learning. It is about internalising, adapting and then practicing.

We must all be performers; that is part of a leadership role. But the same part can be played many ways – sometimes achieving power in an understated way, sometimes in a bold interpretation, occasionally surprising by using a voice that is not ordinarily your own. That is what makes great theatre, and it also makes great leadership. I have probably seen forty different actors play Hamlet, and with the best of them I see something new. Recently I saw the versatile actor Patrick Stewart play Claudius, and his interpretation was as if I had never seen the part played before. You can achieve the same thing – in a town hall meeting or in a brainstorming session – if you make people feel that they are seeing you perform fresh and for the first time.

WEEK 41

Competencies and Skills

We all know what skills are. They are, effectively, expert knowledge that a person acquires through learning and practice. An employee may have all the skills required to open a new pizza restaurant in a chain. He knows how to secure the real estate, get the equipment and furniture ordered, hire the key staff, secure the appropriate training so it meets the chain's standards, and check on the quality both in the first week and later after opening.

But does he have the competencies required to do this first responsible job successfully? Having hired the key staff, can he quickly build them into a team? Is he astute enough to understand the relationships that need to be built with other local merchants? Will he be able to motivate the new store manager to achieve exceptional performance? How does he react to change in the business environment? And beyond all that, does he have the competencies to think through what the future strategy is on opening new stores?

If he has ideas, will people listen to him? If he is put in charge of a bold new venture (say, expanding the pizza chain network to Uzbekistan), will he be able to build the team to carry it out successfully? Even if he can build that team, will it align behind him or go in several different directions.

Skills and competencies are two very different things, and it is the astute corporation that recognises this and thinks deeply about it. When you hire new graduates or junior employees, when you train them and promote them through the lower grades (assuming we have grades, see Week 31) you are mainly doing so based on how well they acquire and practise the skills they need for the job.

At the same time you can appreciate that the skills required to be really excellent at one level may be much less important at the next level. Investment banking Analysts, the entry level position, must be really good these days at using spreadsheet programs like Excel. They often have to produce complex models for deals in a short time under enormous pressure, and if there are errors these can be very costly to the firm.

But go up one level, to Associate in an investment bank, and there is already some direct dealing with clients, not through your boss but on your own. Now the skill is in checking the Analyst's spreadsheet, being sure the assumptions are correct, suggesting variations to see what the sensitivities are.

At the Vice President level, which is the next level up for investment bankers, much more time is spent with his own clients, and relationships with other members of the firm –

bringing together the different sorts of expertise required to win a client or do a deal successfully – come to the fore.

Here, as in most businesses, as a person progresses, she develops and expands her skills, but also starts to need new competencies. Think of competencies as fitness. Indeed, they are fitness for purpose. Unless we have this fitness we will not practise our skills effectively. I think this is pretty clear to all of us in the pizza restaurant example: we have probably all seen someone who had mastered every skill required to do a job like this, but still made a total mess of it because they lacked the required competencies.

A possible set of competencies that were used in BP is shown in the 3 x 3 grid below. There is nothing about these that should be viewed as prescriptive. Each company can figure out its own, and should do so. Indeed, the process of coming to these involved a lot of interviews with leaders of the company at several levels, to see what they considered to be important, both to success of the company, *and* to being successful in the company, alignment of these two being crucial.

Respected Player	Acts Wisely and Decisively	Leads Change
Strategic Influencer	Builds Best Teams	Shapes Performance
Strategic Conceptualizer	Environmentally Astute	Ensures Alignment

While maintaining that each company will have its own competency framework, I would suggest that, for senior leadership, it must include something about strategic ability, something about team building, awareness of what is going on around you external to the company, and ability to execute. I was struck by an analysis done in 1999 by *Fortune* magazine on 'Why CEOs Fail', which concluded that it is not often due to a failure of strategy but more to failure of execution. So core competencies for leadership are about strategic thinking, ability to influence and to execute.

It is pretty easy to teach skills and to evaluate how well these skills have been learned. It is much harder to develop competencies and to evaluate how well these are practised. Some leaders seem to operate on the assumption that skills are taught but you have to be born competent – 'either you got what it takes or you don't'. I disagree. I know that my own competencies have developed a lot over my management career, some through courses I have taken, some through being observant, a lot through receiving feedback and acting on that feedback. Competency development for an up and coming staff member is why we think carefully about the assignments they are given, and with whom they will be working on these assignments.

Not everyone can be raised to the highest level of skills in a particular area, nor can everyone be developed to the highest level of competency required to lead a major corporation. But it is in the interest of the corporation to develop everyone to the highest level at which they can contribute. Failure to invest in doing this is the biggest area of waste that most companies have.

WEEK 42

One Management System

The 20th century was a great period for developing organisational structures and systems. Some companies found one of these that worked for them and their leadership, evolved it over time, and then stuck with it. Others were more experimental. In the later part of the 20th century and early in the 21st, companies like Apple, Google, and Facebook tried radically different approaches to their management systems.

Merging of two companies means sorting out how the company is going to be managed, who is going to manage it of course, but more importantly how. We all know that there are lots of different systems – business units, regional organisations, functional groups, highly centralised control, highly dispersed services, etc. And none of these is demonstrably the right way or the wrong way.

What all this means is that only rarely will two merging companies have the same management system. When companies merge they must try to be appreciative of *what* is good and *who* is good in each other's companies. But that does not apply to the management system. From the outset, after any major corporate merger, it must be made clear that the new company can only have one management system. It does not have to be either one or the other system exactly replicated, but it has to be a clear system, that everyone can understand, and certainly not a hybrid. Why? Because the hybrid system would not be something you would ever choose if you were designing a company, and it would only be used because it represented parts of two specific companies. A bad idea.

This is a surprisingly common failure in mergers (much less so in acquisitions, especially of smaller into larger companies), and one that is so easily avoided. And all the work to decide how the company will work can be done in advance of the actual completion of the deal, written down, and understood by all the key players.

Some people will not like the outcome. That is inevitable. We get very attached to our way of doing things. If these people dislike the new way enough, they don't belong in the new company, and the sooner they realise that the better.

FOR THE WEEKEND

Leap Backward into the Future

When I came to the UK in 1988 to work for BP I was rather depressed by what I found. I was running a division at the Research Centre at Sunbury, and my administrative assistant told me that lunch was the highlight of his day. What's more, he told me that his ambition was mainly to last long enough to be admitted to the 'Senior Mess' on the basis of longevity. At the Research Centre there were two levels of dining, the Junior Mess and the Senior Mess. To eat in the Senior Mess you had to reach grade 12, but if you were Grade 11 with 25 years of service then you could also 'become a member' of the Senior Mess. Two of my Senior Mess colleagues told me that the biggest problem at Sunbury was that there was to be a woman member of the Senior Mess, the first ever (and this was in 1988!). Just why I should see this as a major tragedy was not clear, but they certainly did. Then there was the Staff Consultative Committee I had to chair, an elected group who put questions to management on things that were bothering the staff. At my first meeting I learned that they were very concerned about the problem of staff not being allowed both a hot pudding and ice cream at their lunch (which, by the way, was free). It is certainly a bad sign when so much of what is on people's minds is lunch.

All that was a bit sad. Then an attempt by the Chief Operating Officer of the Research Centre to get me involved with an 'important committee' in the Corporate Centre only gave me further exposure to bureaucracy gone more than a little bit mad. I am sure the committee actually did something, but I cannot recollect anything about the meetings except that most of the time was spent going over matters arising from previous meetings, some of which went back several years. This committee had the job of helping to place people who were promising young talent (but perhaps not the most promising, destined for the Board) in new roles. It was difficult for the Committee to accomplish anything – not just the actions which were carried forward and considered but rarely carried out – it was also that as usual there was a senior HR person who was staff to the committee, and he played a very devious role in the whole thing. A name would be brought up, and someone would say he (always a he) was a very good manager, had done an excellent job on such and such a project, etc. And the HR guy would say something like 'Yes, very good man, can be difficult, can be difficult, but still . . .' and that would pretty much kill off anyone's interest in having that person in their organisation.

The state of information technology and communications technology in BP in 1988 typified the problems of the place.

The phones were primitive, email hardly used (though in the US the whole company was already using email for all communications) and attitude towards change was hostile. A consultant came around to talk to me about modernising the phone system, and asked what I wanted. I replied that something like what I had at a summer job in New York in 1961 would be a great advance.

When I proposed at a meeting of the directorate of the Research Centre that we use electronic communications to prepare the annual plan, rather than walking around end-less drafts of documents (most of which were unnecessary anyway) the Director of Research told me that it was not my job to suggest changes, that he did not believe in email, and that he had talked to some of his friends at other com-panies and they didn't believe in it either. This from the head of R and D at a company that thought of itself as one of the leading industrial enterprises of the world! Of course, he got the usual result that you get when you block sensible change from the top: the younger leaders in the Research Centre just changed to email and didn't ever tell him or his associates about it, so they were left out of all the communication and discussion until we had finalised the plan among ourselves.

On the bureaucracy problem, change came quickly. When Bob Horton returned to BP from his time in the US he realised how bad things were. During his years in the US, running BP America, he saw how people would talk to him about what they wanted to do, take action, and get things done, and he moved to streamline the organisation (Week 8. Clutter). The different levels of dining also disappeared, though at the Research Centre this only happened by getting the Director of Research out of his job.

The IT problem was less tractable. Most of the leadership of the corporation had degrees in History or Arts subjects, and were inherently uncomfortable around computers. They saw the computer as an innovation that required executives to type, and they did not type; that was women's work. Not to mention filing. A consultant came in to work on modernising the corporation in terms of IT, and when he presented to the executives on the Board on how they as individuals had to change, one of the Board members got up and walked out. The corporation really had to be dragged into this.

John Browne was a Physics graduate from Cambridge and approached this differently (though I don't know that he ever typed answers to emails himself during his tenure as CEO, and possibly not to this day). I recall during the early days of the explosion of internet access and content, several of us started to press for the idea that BP needed to have a website for communicating with all sorts of constituencies. I know the idea that anyone would think otherwise is incomprehensible today, but that was not the case 15 years ago. John convened a meeting to talk about it, and heard objections from some senior executives about how we would lose control of valuable information, etc. Then he started asking questions about how the internet was being used. I mentioned that I read the *New York Times* each morning on my computer by accessing their website. He looked at me for about 15 seconds and then said, 'Well, I think we must have a website too' – and that was that.

WEEK 43

Experience Counts

It is often said that all the great advances in mathematics are made by mathematicians in their 20s or early 30s. Many of the advances in physics are also done by the youngest scientists. By contrast, in chemistry a lot of great work is done by chemists in their 50s and 60s. Whereas mathematics and physics are disciplines where the big problems are well known, and the trick is not to be hindered by all previous attempts to solve them, chemistry is a science where the ability to integrate a wide array of knowledge is required to see where the big opportunities lie. Much of what is done in big companies, in mature industries, is more like chemistry than mathematics and much of what is done in the venture capital/start up world is more like mathematics than chemistry.

Sometimes the modern corporation makes it a priority to get rid of the older employee. There are lots of good reasons for this. Pension structures can be one. Another is that if the workforce is constant or shrinking overall, only by pushing people out at the top end of the age range can you do any hiring of new talent.

This certainly makes sense. Companies have developed and used various incentive plans to persuade people to retire early. But is this really desirable from the viewpoint of actually carrying out the business?

I think that today we undervalue experience. Perhaps not in the go-go businesses of Silicon Valley, where there is precious little experience available. But in the mature businesses – oil, chemicals, minerals, retailing, pharmaceuticals, and many others. In these businesses experienced employees can and do make the difference between success and disaster.

Nobody learns the lubricants, the acrylonitrile, the gold production business, or how to steer a new drug through trials until it reaches the market, at university. No one really learns how to deal with customer complaints, especially those from trade customers, in a classroom. We essentially learn this stuff by an apprentice method, younger employees learning from older ones, getting the freedom to do things unsupervised, and then doing them year in and year out for a few decades. The value that an experienced member of a team brings to a mature business, assuming he or she is operating effectively in the team context, is huge.

Who is responsible for determining whether expertise, hard won over decades, is retained or lost to the company? You might argue that it is not the senior leadership of the corporation making the decision to retire this person early. But it is, of course it is. By indicating to the Business Unit

Leaders that they have to take out so many staff, and putting in place, via HR, the incentives that make it attractive for older, more experienced employees to go, the leadership of the company does make these decisions.

As I said, they may be the right decisions, and in the long term good for the company. But let's be sure we listen to our team leaders about consequences, and put in place the kind of training for younger employees that backs up a decision to shift the workforce away from experienced staff. Let's be sure that we are thinking about both the short and long term, evaluating everyone in a meritocratic system commensurate with their age and experience. Finally, let's educate managers at all levels to progressively enhance the roles of experienced employees so that they take on accountability for developing future generations of experienced people for the corporation.

WEEK 44

Searching for Stars

When I joined Sohio, at an advanced age (43) for a new entrant, I was told that before joining I would attend an assessment centre, or at least a mini version of one, where my potential for senior management would be evaluated. Well, I was a good academic, so I did a little research on such things, and found articles in Harvard Business Review about assessment centres in companies such as JC Penney and AT&T. In JC Penney one of the competencies they were looking for was customer responsiveness, and to assess this, participants would receive phone calls in the middle of the night from actors playing the role of irate customers, with their approach being evaluated. I can't recall anything about what I learned of the AT&T one, though that probably involved something with telephones as well.

What I attended at Sohio was not terribly interesting, mainly consisting of a battery of mathematical and verbal reasoning tests, along with some psychological testing and interviewing. This was not really an assessment centre, although I later learned that the senior management of Sohio believed that the mathematical and verbal reasoning tests had great predictive ability for successful leaders. I somehow doubt this was ever verified by evidence – rather it was one of those prejudices it is more comforting not to try to test. Some years later a firm convinced BP to give all of its senior managers a similar set of aptitude and psychological tests, with equally useless results.

But assessment centres, real assessment centres, are much more fun and much more useful. They involve taking a peer group of employees away for a few days, where they carry out a series of exercises, individually and in groups, in the presence of observers. The classic individual exercises are 'the inbox', in which the individual takes action on a full array on incoming paperwork (probably by now the inbox is electronic anyway), and 'the difficult employee', in which an actor plays an employee who is causing problems on a project or within a team.

In the group exercises, there is usually a problem of some sort to be solved – a missed production schedule, a decision on an investment, something where individuals are not assigned but rather find their roles. Some people become very operational, others very strategic. Some try to dominate the conversation, others fade into the wallpaper. These exercises can be very revealing, but the observers must be skilled and perceptive in order to see what is revealed.

In the best version of this that we ran in BP, the exercises had been professionally designed to give participants a chance to demonstrate the competencies that BP felt were important in its senior leadership. It is very important that competencies rather than skills are being judged, because specific job experiences give people skills, but competencies are transcendent. The observers see all the participants in different situations, and note down what they see. Only after all this is complete do the observers, led by a professionally trained facilitator, sit together and share their observations. Finally, having heard and discussed this, they decide what this means in terms of the observed competencies of the individual participants – fully up to expectations for this level, needing improvement, or far off the standard.

All of this is then fed back to the individuals, and becomes input to the committees at senior level that look at development assignments for key employees.

Well, if this all sounds like a time consuming and expensive process, you are right, it is. But if it works, if it identifies from among a talented pool those individuals who are really suited for broad senior leadership roles in a big corporation, then surely it is worth it.

Moreover, in my experience, the assessment centre as I observed it in operation did three other things well. It identified employees who were thought of as good but not extraordinary, but who shone in the assessment centre. In several cases this result led to more challenging job assignments for these people, which some of them carried out with distinction. It probably only takes one of these results every now and then to pay back an investment in the assessment centre for a large corporation.

The second good outcome was to highlight employees who were really good at what they did, but who did not have the potential to work more broadly. The superb trader, lawyer, engineer, or scientist. When the assessment centre worked well, the feedback to individuals at the end of the week along these lines was generally very well received.

And third, the centres are a developmental tool for the observers, drawn from senior management, trained very quickly by professional staff, who then spend days observing and long hours discussing what they have seen. In the corps of observers there develops a much deeper understanding of what the competencies, heretofore just words on a chart (Week 41. Competencies and Skills) really mean to the corporation. They have an opportunity to spend a week working with peers from across the corporation on a meaningful task, and they become well acquainted with a number of promising staff who they may be mentoring in their careers.

Can you find your stars through assessment centres? Yes, but first you have to have a very good idea of what sort of competencies a star in your corporation will have. If you have not reached consensus on that, how can you possibly assess individuals? Second, you have to invest in doing it professionally, and recognise that a substantial up-front investment and ongoing investment of time is important.*

---

* There are firms that specialise in running assessment centres for multiple companies, and if your company is a small to medium sized one this could be the right path to take. The positives are that you will learn whether your employees are as good as or better than those of other companies; while you are not assessing them against your own particular set of exercises, it may not matter, since companies are not all that different anyway; and you don't fall into the traps of looking for clones of your current management, or of thinking that you know what a person needs to be successful

Senior leaders in the corporation need to participate as observers, and that means they have to commit to blocks of time, including time for training.

This required role of senior management as observers, at least once, goes right to the top of the company. Unless the people who are going to look at the outputs of the assessment centre have been through the process as observers, they will not be able to interpret the reports and evaluations coming out of it with intelligence and understanding. So: expensive and time consuming? Yes. But can there be any more important use for our time and money than identifying our future leaders and their development needs?

– the assessors will give you an objective view of this. This could be the most cost effective way of doing the assessment. The negatives are that you might not do the hard thinking about what your firm really requires in terms of competencies, you don't rigorously test people against those specific competencies, you don't get your senior leadership involved in the process (although some external firms will provide for this as a possibility) and, to me, most important, you don't bring your corporate values to bear on the assessment.

WEEK 45

The Leader as Teacher

I frequently thought of staff meetings, even the more senior level executive committees, as rather boring chunks of time in my work week. Sure there are things that need to be communicated, and items to be decided, but once these things are set up as regular occurrences, week in and week out, they tend to degenerate into unstimulating lists of agenda items to be got through.

But when I worked at Sohio, I spent some time working for Ron McGimpsey, who led the refining and supply side of the business at that time. He showed me that the meeting – in this case it was monthly – was really an opportunity to teach and learn. I think many great leaders use executive committee meetings this way.

I recall one meeting we had with Ron, where we had wound up with a surplus of product in one part of the State, and had suffered on prices. Rather than just rueing the events that had led to that, or chastising the manager who had erred, he took the time to say: OK, let's understand how we got into this mess, how we get out of it, and most important, how stop it happening again. We worked together for an hour or so on this, as a group, until we all understood it deeply.

I thought: now that was really valuable, that was something where we all walked away from discussing what was a bad result and had a good outcome.

Another time, where someone – perhaps it was me – was advocating that we take a strong position on methanol as a fuel for vehicles, and do so in a way which would have been public, Ron stopped and suggested that before doing that, let's understand why we have long taken a different position, and does this still hold, and if it does let's be sure we all understand the rationale for that position. But also, we should understand the difference between questioning our position internally and challenging it externally.

It may seem a luxury to take time out to explain and teach in this way. I don't think so. Rather it is the way in which today's leader develops the future leadership of the company, and the way that a deep understanding of principles, strategy, and culture are embedded in management. Done well, at all levels, it is as good a use of time as there is for a corporate leader.

WEEK 46

Balanced Scorecard

The word balance can mean many things. We say 'our life is in balance' when we have a good mixture of work, love, community. We say 'our life hangs in the balance' when there is a danger that removing one element, or tripping one switch, will end it. As a chemist, I learned to use the two pan balance to weigh small quantities of chemicals, adding small weights, so tiny that a fingerprint would give an erroneous result, until the needle stopped in the centre of its swing. I understood how sensitive the process of balance could be. Similarly as children we sit on the seesaw, our friend sits on the other end, and we try to get it to stop, perfectly balanced.

The idea of balanced scorecard comes from an evolution of thinking about the balance of business objectives at the corporate or business unit level. It can be applied to individuals, but it is really an idea about the objectives of the entire management: What are we trying to achieve as a company? There was a time, and perhaps it still exists in some smaller companies, appropriately even, where the objectives were very simple: Sell x amount of product and do it profitably. Grow sales. Take market share. Enhance margin. Manage the cash. The business of the company is business, and that is about money. The bottom line.

Then some years ago, mostly as a result of external pressure – from shareholders, maybe from customers, from regulators, from NGOs – companies started to say, there need to be some non-financial objectives as well. Sometimes it was the Board that pushed management in this direction; sometimes the Board did not see this need as clearly as management. So companies began, maybe 20 years ago, to see the formula for rewarding the CEO and senior executives as a combination of achievements against the financial and non-financial objectives, something like 75% on financial objectives, 25% on non-financial, such as customer complaints, environmental protection, employee turnover, things like that.

From this evolved a very useful idea, namely the balanced scorecard. What it says is this: as a corporation, we have to accomplish a number of things, in broad categories. Meet the business plan; keep employees safe, healthy and motivated; protect and enhance the communities in which we operate; care for the environment; operate within the law. Different for every corporation, to be sure, but broad categories such as these. Within these categories, one can have annual objectives, such as reducing lost time incident rate (safety) by 10%; reducing absenteeism by 15%; reducing our emissions to air and water below the average of any country in which we operate; targeting community support through creation of a community arts panel; and of course, increasing profit before tax by $10 million, reducing operating costs so that we eat inflation. And when the corporate leadership, together with the Board, can agree that these objectives, somewhere between say five and twenty of them, are what the company needs to accomplish to be successful, that these are the targets and these are the stretch targets beyond the base, then this can be the basis for reward – salaries, bonus, stock, whatever is appropriate. But more important, these objectives are the implementation of strategy, the clear focus on what the company is trying to execute.

Now one way of thinking of this as a balanced scorecard is that it includes the major elements that are important to the company's key constituencies – shareholders, employees, customers, regulators, community. That is the way I think most people see the idea of balance in this scorecard. But there is another. When you use this scorecard, live with it for a while, you inevitably find that sometimes you have to sacrifice something to achieve something else. Not every target can be sacrificed as easily as every other. You cannot compromise safety, or environmental protection, or ethical behaviour, to improve profits. But sometimes you have to sacrifice your goal on, say, operating costs to reduce emissions, or to achieve a regulated outcome that was more difficult than you thought it would be. Sometimes you have to take a hit on employee motivation in order to redesign work patterns that are more efficient and effective. It is when balance takes on this meaning that management is called upon to make the most difficult judgements, and, I hope, earns the admiration of the Board.

WEEK 47

If You Can't Manage Safety, You Can't Manage

Russell Seal, who led BP Oil for many years, used to say 'If you can't manage safety, you can't manage' and I believe this to be true. If you cannot run a business, any business, in a way that protects the lives and limbs, the eyes and hearing, and the health of your employees then you cannot run that business. Simple as that.

Any CEO who allows a business unit in his company to run with a poor safety record is not asking the right questions. Any Board that allows its company to run with a poor safety record is not doing its job either. So what exactly is poor? Is it worse than average? For our industry, for our country? What is the standard?

I am sure that the only appropriate goal is no accidents whatsoever. It is never enough to say 'we are doing better than others'. Safety is an absolute, not a relative corporate value. And while one does not go from poor performance to zero accidents in an instant, or even in a year, it is the goal that has to be firmly set and always kept in view, no matter the starting point.

Safety needs to be the first item on the agenda, and on the Agenda. It is the first thing to think about when you are asking 'how are we doing?' or talking about that to a town hall meeting, it is the first thing to talk about at an offsite conference or when visitors are present at a meeting ('if there is an alarm, it will sound like a continuous bell, we will leave by the stairway to the right of the door, and assemble in the car park') and at a management meeting or a CEO Board report it is absolutely the first thing to cover (accidents, investigations, near misses). Having safety at the front of mind in your business mentality will spread to your home repairs, and to travel safety, for example routinely checking how you will get out of your hotel room in case of a fire alarm.

Radical improvement of safety performance happens if you pay attention. Without management attention, it drifts. As much as anything in a corporation, yes, as much as strategic direction and financial performance, safety performance reflects corporate leadership. And this needs to be sustained over time, not for days or weeks or months, but forever. But why is this?

I think there are two simple reasons. First, because while employees don't come to work wanting to be injured, or killed, they are people and people take shortcuts. Have you ever seen a lawn that people did not cut across if they were able to? And shortcuts, bred in the soup of repetition and familiarity, lead to accidents. Not isolating an electrical system because the operation to clean a trap has been done every week for years, and there was never a problem. Leaving the motor running on a truck while you go up to turn off a valve, because you want to get back to the control room quickly on a freezing cold night. Not putting on a seat belt for a short drive.

Second, because as the leader, you put in place actions to improve safety and it improves to a certain level. I can guarantee you that if you start with a mediocre performance, you will improve, which is good and satisfying, but then you will plateau at a somewhat better performance. When you are on that plateau, more actions are required, in addition to what you are already doing, to get to a better plateau. And so on, until you get to a point where year after year there are no accidents. Even to sustain this exceptional performance requires constant attention, refreshing, and curing of small problems before they become big ones. The processes that a company of any size uses to improve and sustain superb safety performance are for all times.

'No accidents' in manufacturing industries means that every bit of the plant is running safely, of course. But it also means that if someone spills a teaspoonful of coffee it is wiped up at once, before someone else comes along and slips on it. That the kitchen operates to the same set of standards as the plant, that the back office has the same standards of housekeeping as the factory.

Even if there is no factory, only office, everyone is conscious of having a safe working environment. Indeed, if the company you are leading consists only of retail stores and deliveries, safety consciousness is just as important as if you are running a dynamite factory.

'No accidents' is at the bottom of a staircase that we walk down through our rules, statements, actions, improved skills, and unrelenting attention. And when a setback occurs, as they will, we regroup, we look for root causes, we reinvigorate what we were doing, and re-establish our place on the staircase.

FOR THE WEEKEND

Discipline and Focus

Always in a successful career you have to work and work, then work some more. But also learn lessons about focus.

I became an assistant professor at Hunter College, part of City University of New York, in 1967. I had been in Switzerland for a year, as a postdoctoral fellow at the Swiss Federal Institute of Technology, known as the ETH for its German initials, one of the three or four greatest places for science in the World. Getting a job from abroad was not easy, but after a week in the US in March I had three job offers, of which Hunter was probably the second best. My wife, Elly, wanted to be in New York for her graduate education, and it was fine for me. As it turned out, Hunter and CUNY were, to some extent, on the way up, and an exciting place to be for many reasons. What I thought was the best job offer I had was from a NASA lab in Cambridge, Mass. That lab was actually closed by the government a couple of years later, which would have left me looking for a job in the early 70s, one of the worst times for a young PhD to be unemployed.

I wrote a proposal to the American Chemical Society for a small grant to do some studies on liquid crystals, and, somewhat to everyone's surprise at Hunter College, I got the grant. The university gave me some additional equipment money as a reward – when you are at a place like Hunter where new faculty getting grants was not an everyday occurrence, the Deans were apt to be generous. So there I was, with a little office, a lab, some basic equipment, and lots of teaching to do, trying to write a proposal for a bigger grant, and basically my own hands and time to get some research done.

Before long a few undergraduates gravitated to me to do some part time research, and I had the beginnings of a lively little group. I wrote a proposal to the American Cancer Society then, for research on the fundamentals of cell membranes, building on the ideas of liquid crystals. This time, with a little coaching, I got the Deans to precommit to some more significant additional funding in support of the proposal if it was awarded. They certainly did this in the expectation I would be turned down. Once again, sometime in autumn 1968, I received the grant. Now I had enough to get started, and my first couple of graduate students were working with me.

But I did something very wrong at the beginning. I had money, equipment, students, and lots of ideas. Too many ideas as it turned out. What resulted was a nice group of students working on all sorts of experiments off the main line of my proposals. Sure, we published a lot of papers on one big subject, and these were good papers, published in first-rate journals that got the attention of my little part of the scientific community. I won some awards, had lots of invitations to speak, etc. so what was wrong with that? Simply that we also spent a lot of time away from the most impactful area, wasted manpower, time and intellectual effort too.

I saw this pattern repeated by many of my colleagues in universities, and I see it over and over again in industry. Focus is everything, but at the same time it is anathema to the curious intellect of people. We keep seeing interesting paths to wander down, and take them even when the main goal will be so much more rewarding.

Besides being distracted on my research, I also allowed myself to be distracted by other things. I ran a summer programme for a group of high school teachers. It was a worthwhile thing to do, for someone to do, but not for someone at an early stage of his career. Publishers pestered me to write a book, and I played with that as well. I lacked discipline, and the ability to say no.

In the end I got a good result from my first eight years as a university faculty member, but I could have had a great result. Discipline and focus were something that had never been a part of my educational experience, or my personal growth either up to that point.

When you are in a position of leadership, focus is of paramount importance. This seems contradictory, after all, doesn't the leader have to work on everything in her span of control, in the case of the CEO the whole company? Yes, but not all the time. For example, as leader you need to be thinking and working on things that could affect the company's success 3, 5, or 15 years out. You need to be doing speeches and meeting people for community relations, or travelling to operations in other parts of the world from where your headquarters are. All these things are important. But the disciplined leader will know that when there is a major acquisition being worked on, or when there is an event that could affect the company's licence to operate, that is the time to strip the schedule of all distractions, remove everything that is important but not urgent, and focus.

WEEK 48

Town Hall

If you have a few hundred people working for you, they want to know what is happening in the company, and, periodically, they want to hear it directly from the boss. For this there is no substitute for a town hall meeting. Saying this I especially mean that sending out an email telling them what is happening does not substitute for meeting the employees face to face. You can send emails to everyone from time to time, and they do communicate facts, but they don't give context, passion, optimism, or any other emotion. They just don't.

So from time to time – and it does not have to be on any sort of a regular schedule – the boss needs to invite everyone to some gathering place, stand up in front, and talk about what is going on. Then he or she has to take questions, pretty much as many questions as there are for as long as people are interested.

Now, having said that it should be done, indeed that

it must be done, how can you do it so that it is really effective? For me, there is only one key to this. You have to communicate what the company wants the employees to know, and at the same time be frank and open with them. In any well run company, at times of change (and most times are times of change, but special changes, for example a merger, a change in how the company is being organised, an unplanned change in the leadership of the corporation, a new approach to controlling costs) senior leadership usually agree a set of key messages, making these available as slides to those who need to communicate them broadly across the company.

All well and good. But if you just stand up there and read those slides you will have zero credibility with the troops. Any leader worth his position will take the messages on the slides, internalise them, contextualise them, and be able to put them across in his own words. He will know what are the things that are really important to his business or division, and what, if left out or not emphasised, will not be critical. Sometimes it is really useful to use the slides provided, and sometimes it is best if they never see the light of day.

I think that using such centrally provided slides probably follows the same rule as the use of slides in other presentations (Week 1. The Abuse of PowerPoint) – if they convey something more effectively than you can do with your own words, for example a chart or a map or some key numbers, then use them. If you are speaking in English before a group of employees whose first language is not English, use the slides. But otherwise, as I've said, it is best to talk rather than show some low information content PowerPoint presentation.

Critically, you need to put your own self into what you say. You need to know when a little cynicism is required, and when some passion behind a new policy is critical to show people that you are personally committed to it. If you always come across as gung-ho about everything that comes from above, you will not have much credibility with the staff. But if you are too cynical, too much of 'we've heard this all before' then you are doing your company and yourself a disservice. Probably you should be moving on to another employer.

This combination of passion and cynicism is a very carefully prepared mixture, and one that takes practice. It needs thought, and for many leaders, at least until sensibilities are finely honed, it suggests that there needs to be someone to bounce ideas off before holding the town hall. In my own experience, I always tried to have a first-rate HR person, who was in touch with what was on the minds of the staff, who also knew my strengths and weaknesses, with whom I could spend time discussing the town hall, and what messages I needed to get across, in advance of the day.

Questions, and their answers, are crucial of course. Employees are great at probing, if they think you are not really convinced of a point or not supportive of the company position. They are also great at sitting on their hands with their mouths firmly shut if they think they will not get a straight answer, or, worse, if they fear reprisal for asking a difficult question. But the boss who can take questions, answer them in a manner that conveys openness and honesty, with occasional use of humour, without pandering to points that she fundamentally disagrees with, but always with conviction, will learn a lot from a town hall meeting. After the meeting, the good HR person will come to you with key points about the questions that were asked, and probably with some informally gathered feedback from staff as they exited the session.

Like many things in this book, conducting a town hall meeting is a skill. It has to be practised, and you have to be severely self-critical of your own performance. This may only happen two or three times a year in a substantial line job, maybe more often in times of crisis or great change, but everyone who has significant line accountability needs to become proficient at town hall meetings.

WEEK 49

How Jobs Change With Career Progress

There is a popular model used by many HR folk that conveys to employees, especially those progressing through a corporation, that at the outset of a career a job mostly consists of technical content (by which is meant specialist content, for example, selling would be technical in this regard), but as one progresses, the technical content is reduced and the managerial content is increased. As the figure below shows, this little model envisions that the total amount of content is constant, but that the balance shifts.

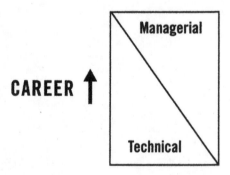

It is so easy for young managers to accept this that I think it must be completely debunked. It is just plain wrong. But why?

First, we all develop as individuals. If we are learning, if we are growing, if we are developing both our skills and our competencies, then we actually are increasing the range of things we can do. Sure, if we were to look at how we spend the hours of a work week, more of them might be spent on tasks which would be viewed as managerial, and fewer on things viewed as technical. But that is not very relevant. Our productivity per hour has increased and the range of work we accomplish should have radically broadened.

What is relevant is that the assembly of skills and competencies that we need to do the job well at any stage of a career changes. And that brings me to a second fallacy. That the technical content goes down. I think that as you progress throughout a career you exchange a requirement for technical depth with a demand for technical breadth.

The CEO or COO does not need to know how to solve key flow equations in a plant, or how to construct a spreadsheet of the monthly results of that plant. But he or she does need to know what the plant makes, how it makes it, what are the key elements of the corporation's technical edge, and what could put these at risk. In a big company, there are many technologies (broadly defined, this is as true for Walmart as for DuPont) operating, and the CEO needs to understand each and every one of these at some level – enough to be able to ask the right questions, make informed strategic as well as operational decisions, and see what is or could be a risk to results.

He or she needs to be able to speak convincingly to the investor community about the business, not just in a managerial way, but in a way that demonstrates command of the breadth of technology for the business.

Of course leadership, as this book tries to convey, does involve a lot of learned skills. Everyone who aspires to grow as a leader must be developing these skills, and honing them through practice. But these skills are not best practised when completely divorced from technical understanding. Rather, leadership skills are developed by using them in the technical context of a business. I believe that great leaders who move between very different companies – for example Lou Gerstner, who went from RJR Nabisco to IBM – bring well developed business instincts, and a full toolkit of motivational competencies. But they also know that this is not enough for success. They have the ability to learn, and quickly, the 'technical' aspects of the new business and its global dynamics.

WEEK 50

Pressure and its Consequences

When I became Chairman of AEA Technology, we were probably less than three months away from losing the company. Debt was moving beyond our limits with the bank, we had issued two profit warnings in the space of three weeks, we were overstaffed, the person who was Chairman and CEO had left suddenly, and the two posts split. All of this left our employees with a lot of uncertainty about their futures. This in a business that was all about selling the skills of our employees to solve difficult problems for others.

In this situation, what was the first thing that I said to the new CEO and the Finance Director? It was this: yes we are in trouble, yes we have to take some radical actions to get out of trouble, but no matter what, no matter how difficult things become, you are never to act in any way that is unethical. We don't cheat; we don't lie to each other, to the board, to our investors. Indeed, because we are in trouble we are going to be as rigorous about our ethical behaviour as possible. As a company, and for the three of us as individuals, we will never try to push the boundaries of what is ethical.

If you are a leader, you will know that you have to put people under pressure, sometimes under extreme pressure, to perform. We achieve great things because of that pressure, because we don't approach our jobs casually but with great intensity. But we need to be alert to the possibility that the pressure will cause people to do things that they know are wrong, just because it is the only way they can see to satisfy the boss.

Some years ago, when I headed the Products Division in BP Oil, we were developing a new lubricant product, a project that was high profile and late. It was late because any new lubricant, before it goes to market, must pass a large number of tests, and these are difficult when the product is meeting the highest standards with some new attributes. We had failed a few of these tests first time through. My colleague Tony Roxburgh, as Director of Marketing, knew the sort of pressure the team was under, and he himself was under pressure from our business units to get the product out. In this situation, he had the courage and insight to ask me to form a small independent group to review all the test results, and only when that group was satisfied would he release the product for sale. Because while getting the product to market was a big deal for the team and for him, he realised that there was a bigger deal at stake: the reputation of the company for integrity in its offer.

While leaders have a right, even an obligation, to exert

pressure to perform, they have to think about the consequences of that pressure for the people involved. One of those consequences is the possibility that people will do something that they themselves know is not right, because you have left them no way out. Checks on this happening are, in effect, providing them with a way out, and clear thinking leadership will see that such checks are in place.

There is another consequence of pressure that requires alertness and sensitivity from leadership: the physical and mental health of the team members. Of course you should always be watching this, but when my team is under pressure, perhaps struggling to achieve objectives, I am especially looking for unexplained absences, explosions of temper, team members going off on their own away from colleagues, changes in dress or physical appearance, anything signalling a person not coping physically or mentally. It is useful for a team leader to know if any team members have a history of problems under pressure, but this is not usually something that is shared with the leader by HR or by individuals themselves. Remember also that problems at home can become aggravated in pressure situations at work.

Putting pressure on the team is a tool for leaders to use in order to achieve extraordinary performance. We learn that setting expectations beyond what people believe is possible can lead to great achievements. None of what I have said by way of caution is meant to deter you from using this tool, but as with any tool it must be used with attention to the health and wellbeing of the individual, and the integrity of the corporation.

WEEK 51

Risk

Business is about taking risks, because if you don't take risks you can never grow the business or distinguish yourself from your competitors. But how does the leadership of the company, executive and non-executive, manage those risks to the best advantage of shareholders?

It is sometimes said that, at least in large companies, the most important thing that the board (and particularly the independent or non-executive directors) can do is ensure that risk is properly understood and managed, and I tend to agree with this. So easily said and agreed to, and in my experience so hard to do effectively.

The evidence for ineffectual risk management in big companies is all around us. Even if we set aside large financial institutions, where the examples of poor risk management have dominated the world economy for much of the past decade, the record is poor. Examples are mergers and acquisitions where enthusiasm for the deal overwhelmed

must have the data to allow them to probe this with management.

3. Failing to see correlations. There is an incident in Alaska, and one in Texas, and one in Indiana. Each one is big, but perhaps not big enough to warrant Board consideration as a major risk. But what if there is a correlation, that is, the culture (of safety, or environmental performance, or whatever) or the quality of management throughout the US operations is such that incidents are more likely to occur there than in the rest of the World. The board has a duty to get underneath what is going on, in the process finding correlations that management sometimes fails to see because they are too close to the problem.

4. Substituting slick process for substantive presentation. There are numerous beautiful graphics programs available to management for the risk discussion. The board members get their papers, and there is a big fold out chart in many colours, displaying the risks. There are axes of frequency and size (the right thing to look at, by the way), coloured blobs whose size indicates the scale of the business, different coloured rings indicating the business unit – you get the idea. This chart is a thing of beauty. But I would ask, is it useful as a starter for discussion? It can be, of course. But is a Board member likely to take out this chart at the meeting and say, 'Let's look at risk 16, that one of our tankers leaks oil into the sea' and ask management to explain what

leads this to happen, how technology can mitigate it, are we using that technology everywhere and if not why not?' Or, Risk 2, that there is a problem with the subsidies for our wind power business in southern Europe, asking 'can you give me your views on how the elections next year in Spain, Portugal and Greece will affect this?' In my experience that is not what happens. The beautiful multi-coloured chart comes out, and Board members are lulled into thinking that everything is under control. It isn't. The thing that is under control is use of the graphics program.

5. By allowing quantification to be done superficially, rather than by using experts. Quantified risk assessment is by now a well-established discipline. It enables us to probe questions of frequency and magnitude in a way that gives robust numbers. It requires us to state our assumptions and test these assumptions. And it forces us to accept answers that are sometimes counterintuitive. This is perhaps the most important role, because I usually feel that the risks, their magnitude and frequency, and the mitigation strategies that boards are given are always the intuitive answer, and that can't always be right.

6. By spending time on too many different risks rather than focusing. When a board is given a chart with 25 different risks laid out in living colour, there is no prioritisation to the risk discussion. In some cases Board members prioritise by going to the upper right

hand corner of the chart, presuming that is where
the big, high frequency risks, are being shown, and
concentrate on those. Maybe, but perhaps more
discussion of other parts of the chart would indicate
that the blob representing risk 15 is in the wrong place.
Wouldn't it be better to pick out three or four things,
understand them more deeply, have a real in depth
discussion and arrive at actions that need to be taken
and reported back to the Board?

7. By not devoting enough time to special events.
   Geographic expansion, acquisitions, a bigger capital
   project than you have ever done before, for things
   of this sort the Board needs more than just a project
   presentation where the last slide is about risks. The
   Board would be better off assuming that management
   has understood the business opportunity, evaluated it
   carefully, and now the reason for bringing this to the
   Board at all is to have a discussion of the risks. That
   is the place where the Board has the biggest chance
   of adding value.

8. The Board doesn't see the horse coming up on the
   outside. Fast growing competitors are the biggest
   risk to some businesses, new technologies obsoleting
   your current main product are another. Management
   worries about such things, or someone in the company
   warns about them, but they are not brought to
   the Board for fear that the discussion will not be
   controllable. The real risks are thus hidden away.

We can do this better; Boards all over the world can do this better. But independent directors need to assert themselves to make it happen, because the forces of coloured graphics are strong, and only very strong willed Board members will overcome them.

WEEK 52

We Keep our Promises

When David Simon became Chief Executive of BP, at a time of difficulty for the company, he made a simple promise, which became known a 1 2 5, that is, that the company would reduce its debt by $1 billion a year, would make $2 billion in profit, and would limit its capital spend to $5 billion. Very simple, covering almost all the main drivers for the corporation. Everyone inside and outside could understand it, and could know whether the company had kept its promise.

Not long after that, the Technology leadership of the company was meeting with our managing director, and we talked about the way forward. We had just done a major reorganisation, the entire way we thought about technology in the corporation had changed, and the way we delivered it had been radically altered. We had to ask ourselves 'what do we do to establish credibility for this new organisation in the first year?' The answer was simple to state. 'We are going to make some promises, and then we are going to deliver on those promises. Next year we will make some more promises, and deliver on those. In this way we will build a track record.'

This notion of a company that makes promises and keeps its promises is a very useful one, whether internally or externally. It is at once both a company culture and an ethic that is fundamental to performance. In essence, it is what stands behind the manager – direct report negotiation of specific objectives for the year, the business unit leader–team leader agreement on deliverables, the CEO–managing director negotiation of what his areas of accountability will mean to corporate performance, and of course the commitment to shareholders. It is what allows all of us to go forward with confidence that everyone is committed to delivery, and that once we are agreed, there is not going to be an ongoing negotiation about performance.

Keeping promises is also important in relationships. In 2003 a group of us was in a discussion with senior executives from Ford about a long term change to fuels and vehicles. The Ford guys were concerned that they might come up with their new vehicles and we would not be there at the right time with the fuelling infrastructure to support them. No, we said, that is part of our relationship. We are promising you that we will be there. But how do we know you will do it? Because we always keep our promises.

About the author, Age −75 to 0

In the village of Rzhishchev, not far from Kiev but definitely not of the city, Isaac Bulkin was a tanner who was proficient at making babies. The tanning was his profession. Babies were what he did with Sara Rosenfeld, whom he married when she was just 15. Yankel Rosenfeld, Sara's father, was a shoemaker, and Isaac his leading supplier of leather, so it was natural that he should in turn supply Isaac with a wife. Together Isaac and Sara produced 11 children, all of whom lived to adulthood, a feat requiring both genetics and luck.

The oldest of these children was a son, Meyer, born in April 1870. He was short, more of a Bulkin than a Rosenfeld in build, and not terribly ambitious. The rabbis thought him an interested but below average scholar. Like his father, he fell easily into being a very observant Jew, while his younger brother Simon was more rebellious. When Meyer was in his late teens his marriage to Esther Jaroslav was arranged. The Jaroslavs were shopkeepers, and Esther had worked in her father's cloth shop since she was old enough to see over the counter. She could see the possibility of Meyer drifting into spending days in the yeshiva learning Talmud and not making much of a living. So with a little help from her father, and given Meyer's weak will, she explained to him that he was going to become the leading hat maker for Jews of the Kiev region. Together they learned how to make men's hats, something every Jewish man and boy needed, formal hats, caps, winter and summer hats. And their shop managed to sell enough so that they could live moderately well.

Meyer turned out to be good at producing offspring as well, just like his father. Within a year of their marriage, in November 1891, a first son, Samuel, was born. Esther suffered terribly with that birth, and several miscarriages occurred before her womb seemed to strengthen enough for her to give birth again, this time to a daughter, Golda, in April 1903, and then a year later to a son, Baruch, in August 1904.

But by this time revolution was in the air. Jews had suffered pogroms for decades, but now there was turmoil and uncertainty. All through the region, young men and their families were finding ways to go to America. Meyer had no particular desire to join this movement, but Esther pushed him. Were they going to stay here and be slaughtered? Why shouldn't their children have opportunities to be successful? Meyer's brother Simon, still in his late teens, was already agitating to join the migration. By late 1905 Esther had won her battle to emigrate, and they had enough money to make it to Hamburg, where Meyer, Esther, their three children, and a young cousin (who they represented as being their son) boarded the SS *Amerika* bound for New York.

In New York they found lodgings in a Lower East Side tenement, and Sara started to lay plans to restart the men's hat business. Meyer, with his knowledge of the craft of hat making, found work in a small factory making men's caps. The money from this paid the rent and bought food for the children, not much more. Sam was already a big strapping boy, taller than Meyer and a lot stronger. If his grandmother had been there she would have said that he had the Rosenfeld body. He was learning English on the streets, though at home only Yiddish was spoken.

Almost at once Esther found herself pregnant again, and she worried about money, about their plans, about how they would survive in New York. One Friday, heavily pregnant now, she set about to scrub the kitchen in preparation for Shabbos. It was a hot late summer day, and as she spread the strong lye soap over the floor she swooned and fainted, her face down in the soapy liquid. It was in this condition that Samuel found her in mid-afternoon. He rushed to call a neighbour, but it was too late. She died early that evening, and her baby with her.

Meyer could not cope with three children, two of them very small. The relatives and friends consulted, and agreed the only solution was for the children to be put into a Jewish orphanage until better arrangements could be made.

Samuel stayed in the orphanage for a year, and then went to work. He was strong, and managed to be taken on as an iron worker, building the Manhattan of the 20th century. But Golda and Baruch stayed in the orphanage until late in 1908, when their father remarried, this time to Anna Ropkin, from Vitebsk in Russia. Anna was not a nice woman; there was a reason why at 28 she had never been married. But with the marriage Meyer's younger children could leave the orphanage and come back to the family home, now an apartment in the Williamsburg section of Brooklyn.

Anna was pregnant immediately. Ten months after her wedding she gave birth to a baby girl, Lenore. Anna was not one for old Yiddish or Hebrew names. She called the older girl, Esther's daughter, Gladys, and the boy Ben. She treated them, and Sam when he was home, very badly. It was only 1½ years later that Anna had another child, a boy, who Meyer named Shimon Ilya, but who Anna, with the connivance of the non-Jewish doctor who signed the birth certificate, called Jacob. Three more children, Freda, May, and David were to follow over the next six years.

They were very poor. The apartment was crowded with children, and there was no room to sleep. On many nights Meyer slept on the kitchen table, before he headed off to the little neighbourhood synagogue for morning prayers, and then on to the factory. He did not advance, and remained a cap maker, working at the machines all day for low wages. Cap maker was the occupation recorded on his death certificate.

One Saturday, coming home from the synagogue, Meyer saw a $10 bill lying on the sidewalk. But it was Shabbos, and it was against Jewish law to pick it up. He covered it with a newspaper, hoping it would still be there after sunset. It was, but when his younger brother Dave heard that he had done this he berated him. 'You set the Torah rule that you don't carry money above feeding your family – some Jew you are!' There is another version of this story told about Meyer, how he came into the tenement one day coming home from work, and found a $10 bill lying on the floor in the entrance. It is said that he went from door to door in the building asking everyone whether they had lost the money.

Ben had followed his older brother Sam as a structural iron worker. Their younger brother, now known as Jack (except to his father, to whom he was always Shimon), was a wild boy at school, truant more often than present after the age of seven. He and his friends were known to the police, who took them down to the station to scare them, even showing them some other young hoodlum being beaten with hoses. His younger sister Freda, when she started school, had to live down the reputation that Jack had already made as a Bulkin.

Somehow Jack learned to read and write, even to speak reasonably grammatical English. By his early teens he was taken in hand by one of the young men trying to channel the energy of the wild Jewish youth into sports, and became part of a running club. Now he was on a team, and they competed in races, often on national holidays, down Ocean Parkway in Brooklyn, around Prospect Park, and in Manhattan as well. Jack won some medals and small trophies in these races.

Running was fine, it was fun, but Jack also needed a job. When he was old enough, or big enough to lie about his age convincingly, Sam and Ben got him into work as an iron worker with them. All were members of the Bridge, Structural, and Ornamental Ironworkers Association, a strong union that controlled who could work.

Together the brothers worked on building skyscrapers, including Radio City Music Hall. Jack was the only one of the three selected to work on the building of Rikers Island Prison. It meant a trip to the Bronx on the subway early every morning, where he would catch the ferry from Port Morris that would take the workers out to Rikers Island. On the morning of September 9, 1932, as they approached the dock on the Island, Jack moved to the rail at the edge of the deck, and called up to the captain of the *Observation*, a 50 year old steam powered vessel, to ask him the time. The next thing he remembered was being in the water. Somehow, as a kid, he had learned to swim in the East River, and he managed to swim to the berth and pull himself out of the water. He was lucky. The boiler explosion that had occurred killed 72 of the 127 on board that day. Only six were uninjured and swam to safety, and he was one of them.

The depression was deep and hard, but the brothers had work and made enough money to get by. However, the explosion shook Jack's confidence, and he started to think about how he could get other work. He talked to some of the older men who had been his coaches in the running team. They wanted him to go back and finish high school, but this was not for him. Still, to do anything other than manual labour, even the semi-skilled and well-paid structural iron work, meant getting more education. In 1935 he found out that he could learn to become a farmer if he could put together the $28 fee needed to enrol in the agricultural college at Farmingdale, 60 miles to the east on Long Island. It took him another year, but in 1936 he presented himself for the two-year course. Living on meagre savings, he learned, and enjoyed learning. The course was more practical than written work, but he excelled, and was able to get work at the College to help with his living expenses. He learned how to milk a cow, how to kill a chicken, but more than that, he learned modern methods of disease control, how to measure and increase yields, how to keep accounts, how to buy feed, and how to sell products. And he learned that he loved farming.

Jack's sister Lenore, now known as Lee, had married Irv Pockell, and they had a small farm in Allentown, New Jersey. When the farm next door came up for sale, Jack borrowed money from his brother Sam for a down payment, got a mortgage, and bought it. There was a big old farmhouse, 20 acres of land, and some chicken coops. Within six months he had a going egg farm, and had become a member of The Co-op, a cooperative of Jewish New Jersey egg farmers who sold their product together into the New York market, and shared the dividends. They were socialist businessmen.

What Jack lacked was a wife. He needed someone to cook and clean for him, he needed companionship and he needed sex. And in 1940 he developed a hernia that needed surgery. There was no way he could keep the farm going and be in hospital for a week. He had no help and couldn't afford any. Jack had taken to visiting the Hechalutz farm in nearby Cream Ridge. Here young men and women from New York City, Zionist youth, were being taught farming skills so they could emigrate to Palestine. Jack was six feet tall, blond, strong, independent and attractive. He was not a Zionist, but he was attracted to the place and its spirit. He had farming skills to share, and helped them with their crops. From time to time some of the young men at Hechalutz Farm came over to his farm to help out when there was a lot of heavy work to do.

Among the young women in Cream Ridge was Bea Kotkofsky, from Brooklyn; like many in the group she had taken to using a Hebrew name, Batya. Just 20 years old, idealistic, intelligent. She was a high school graduate from Thomas Jefferson HS in East New York, and had done a year of college at Hunter before quitting and coming out to the farm. Shortly after her 21st birthday, in January 1941, Jack asked her to marry him and she agreed. They were married at the farm on March 16, 1941. Batya came to live on Jack's farm. His sister Lee was not pleased; this decreased Jack's dependence on her, and she reacted coldly to Batya's arrival.

Batya was a virgin on her wedding night; she knew about sex, as something she talked about with other girls, not as something she did. But it was not unpleasant. She understood about the connection between sex and babies, though she didn't know a lot more than that. When she began to feel ill in late July 1941, vomiting in the morning, she went to see Dr Farmer, who lived close by in Allentown. That was how she learned that she was not sick, but that she was pregnant.

Dr Farmer arranged for her to have the baby in St Elizabeth's Hospital in Trenton, where she would be attended by the nuns. When, early in March 1942, with the country now at war, she felt the labour pains that Dr Farmer had warned her about, Jack drove her to the hospital in his truck. A day later, on March 9, 1942 in the early morning hours, after more than 24 hours of labour, she gave birth to a baby boy.

I was that baby.

I was named Bernard Joseph Bulkin. The Joseph was for Batya's uncle Joe, who she loved, and who had died not long before. The Bernard was a compromise. Batya wanted the name Barnett, after her father, who had died of pneumonia when she was only three. Jack thought that Barnett was too feminine a name, a sissy's name. So they settled on something that sounded vaguely similar and to Jack's mind more masculine, and I was Bernard to my parents and relatives, later Bernie to friends and colleagues.

Acknowledgements

This book is full of my observations, stories and biases. For these I take responsibility. I have had the privilege of working closely with a number of great leaders, some of whom are mentioned in the book. But I particularly value the things I learned from George Bugliarello, Sy Scher, Jenny Grasselli, Glenn Brown, Don Anthony, Ron McGimpsey, Russell Seal, Rolf Stomberg, Rodney Chase, David Simon and John Browne. I also learned a lot from people with whom I worked who acted in ways I did not admire. They remain unnamed.

This book had its genesis in a series of lunches and discussions with my colleague Richard Newton. When he decided not to partner with me in its authorship, I went on alone. But several of his good ideas are still in here in various places. I was helped in my writing of this book by useful discussions with Gillian Manus, Kate Owen and Lyn

Lear, all of whom pointed me to the need to include my personal stories along with the leadership lessons.

Many of the chapters appeared in an earlier form as the column *About Leadership* in *The Huffington Post*, and I am grateful to the editors of the Business pages and to all the readers who sent me helpful comments.

And to my wife, Vivien Rose, who put up with me sitting at the keyboard for hours when I could have been doing something else, my thanks.